DISTANZ

Half State

Tolia Astakhishvili

KONTEXT

with Jacksun Bein
and Livia Polanyi

In-Between Worlds in Plasterboard
Matthias Kliefoth

Tolia Astakhishvili's installations fuse places and narratives in three dimensions. Her arrangements, which unfold nested interiors made of plasterboard—combined with sculpture, drawing, painting, sound, video, and writing—create uncanny, often somber settings in which domestic remnants of everyday objects, mementos, debris, and building materials bring the former spirit of the inhabitants back to life. Deploying techniques of compression, superimposition, and defamiliarization, Tolia's built labyrinths challenge our emotions. The arrangements reflect how profoundly memories become imprinted on physical matter, engendering its own—and perhaps altogether contrived—narratives. Meanwhile, her architectures always also possess their own beauty, touching on our realization that the stuff that piles up, condenses, and preserves personal histories, or may sometimes be there for no recognizable reason. In this tension between fragment, trace, and imagination, the works take on a distinctive aesthetic ambivalence: They are at once fragile ruins and poetic storehouses of experience.

The pictures that the artist has arranged and collaged in this book gesture toward an idea of architecture that presents itself above all in discontinuities and accumulations. It manifests the ineluctable instability of the afterlives of objects and the biographies crystallized in them—and thus also raises the question of how this world can be habitable in an age of crisis, autocracy, and discord.

Tolia Astakhishvili's consistently collaborative approach engenders a structure that articulates creative solidarity through the question of authorship and autonomy. For this book, too, the artist chose to work with a collaborator, writer and critic Jacksun Bein. Their fabulous and grotesque narrative sheds mystical light on the "in-between existence" that is no less central to Tolia's spaces—a half-state: neither born nor lifeless and refusing to emerge from the womb. If her opaque installations appear in the book's text-image collaboration like a biography unto itself, unfolding as though in a cocoon, this is evidence of the unique and open-ended cogency of her spatial assemblages. Expanding the discursive space in this volume in our *KONTEXT* series, the scholar Livia Polanyi engages with the artist in textual fragments by email about the power of language and the parameter of time in relation to our memories.

"My reason lives in a house with my doubting."—Jacksun Bein

memory is selection memories

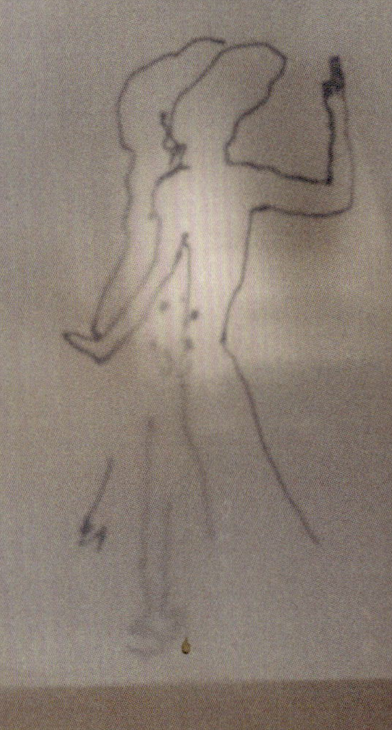
memories

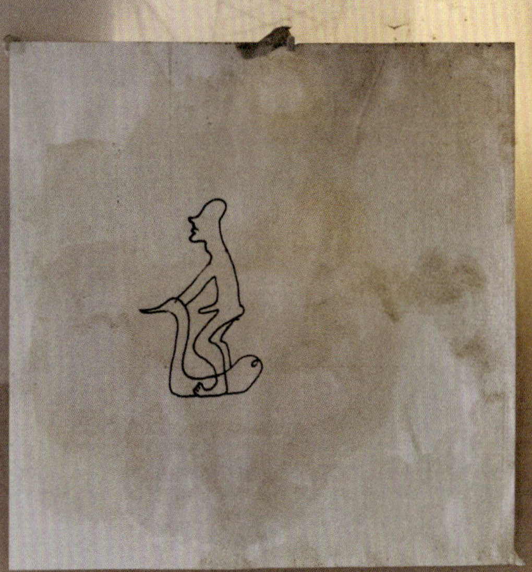

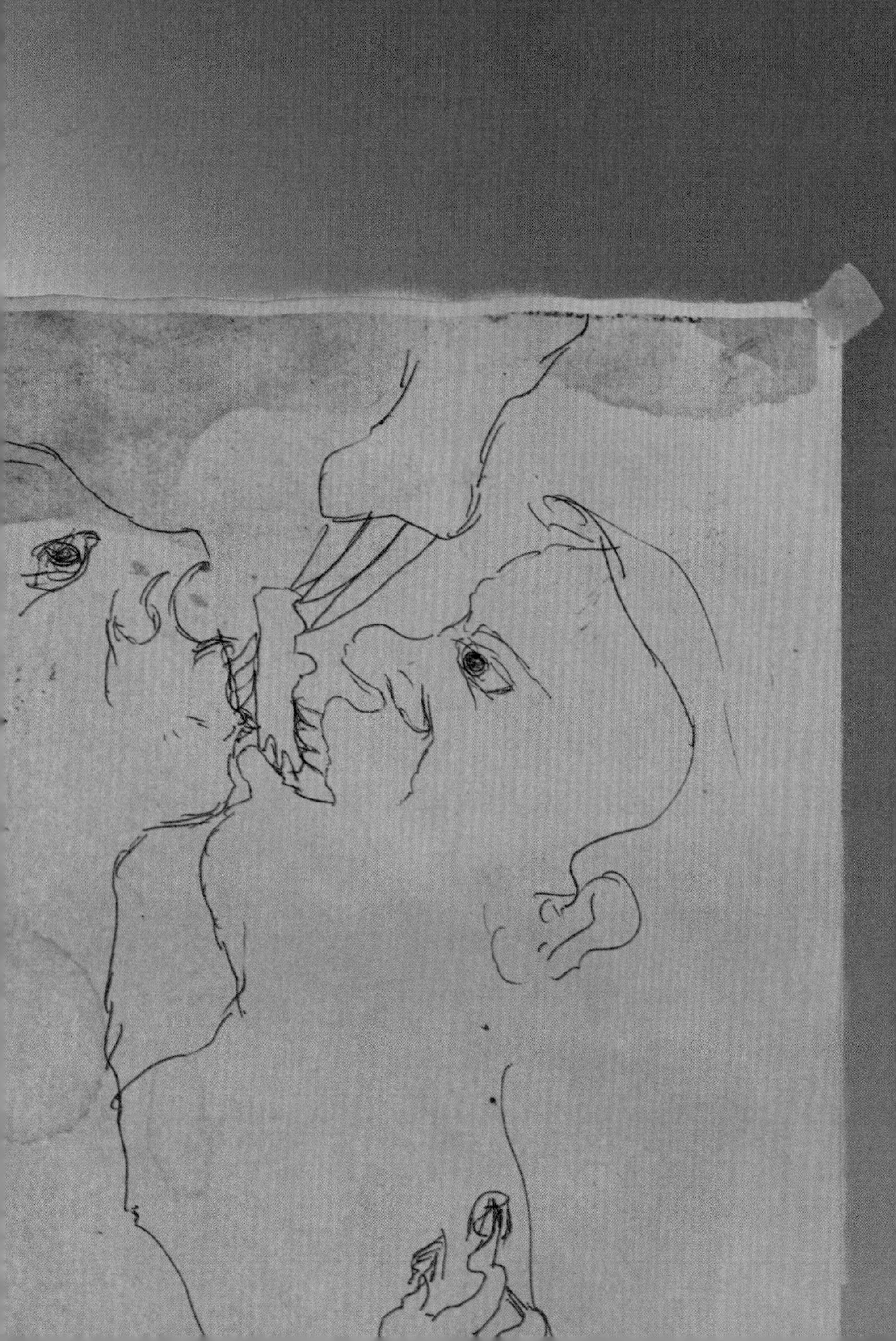

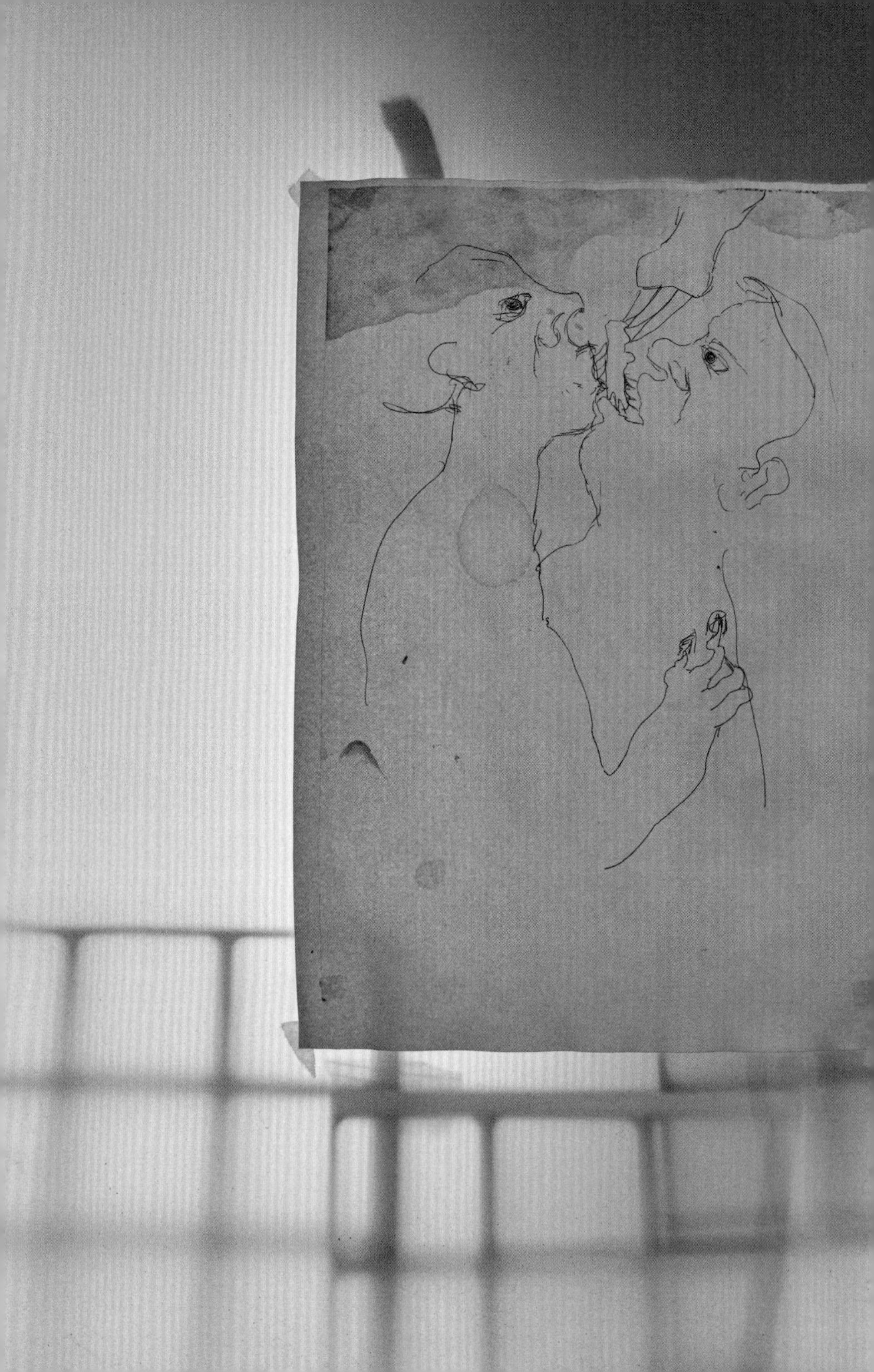

war on my plate.

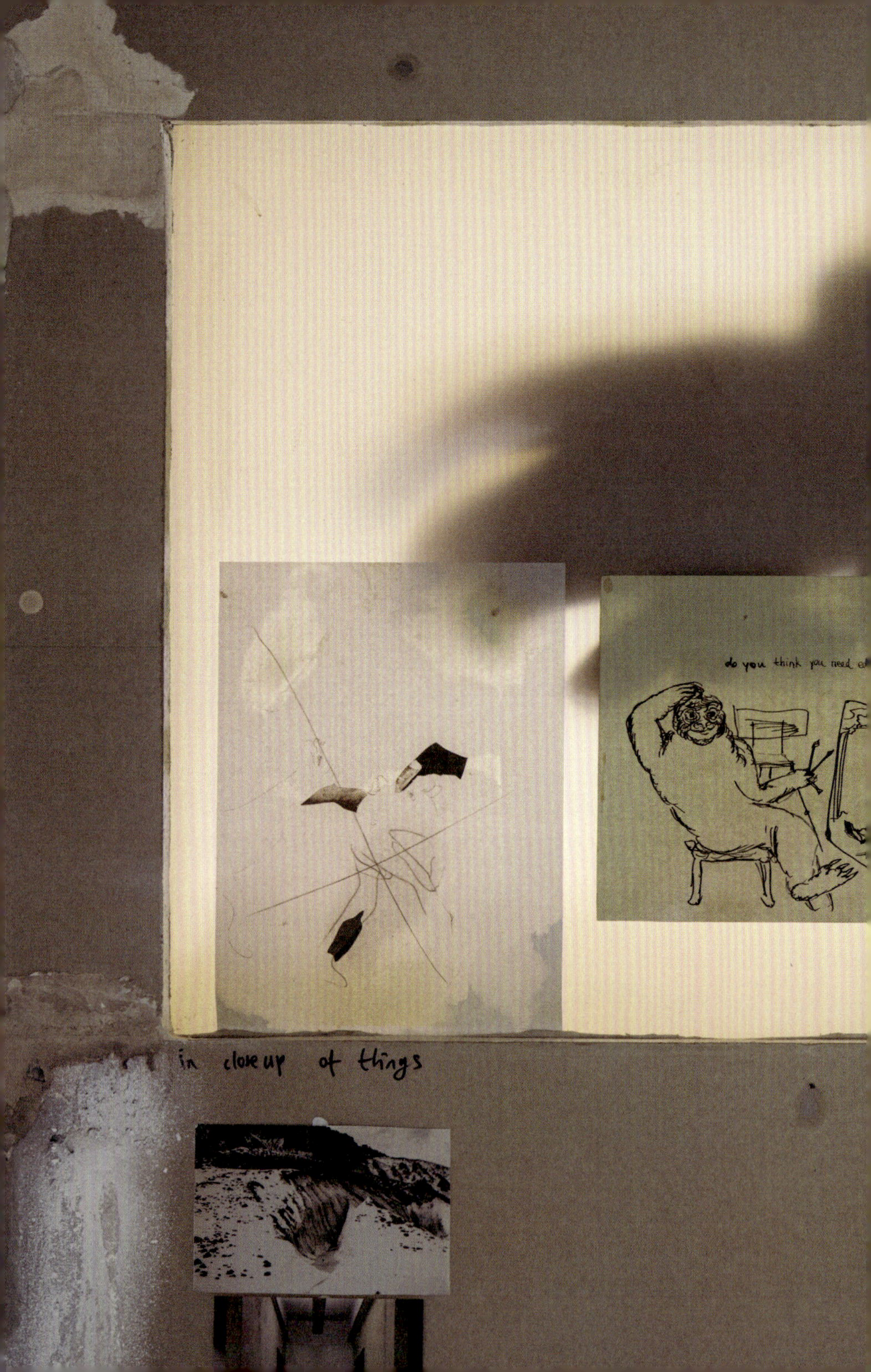

do you think you need

in closeup of things

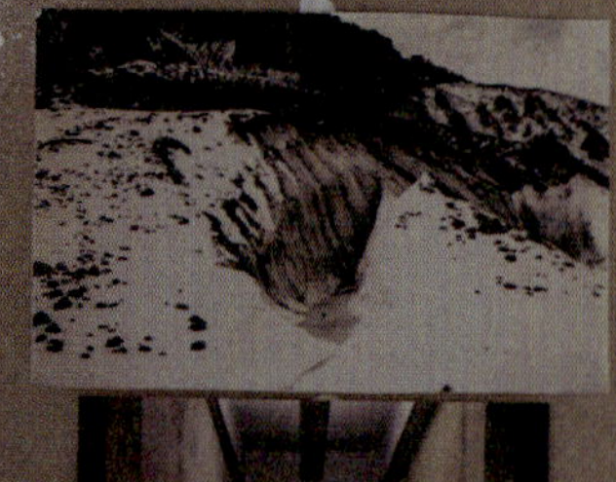

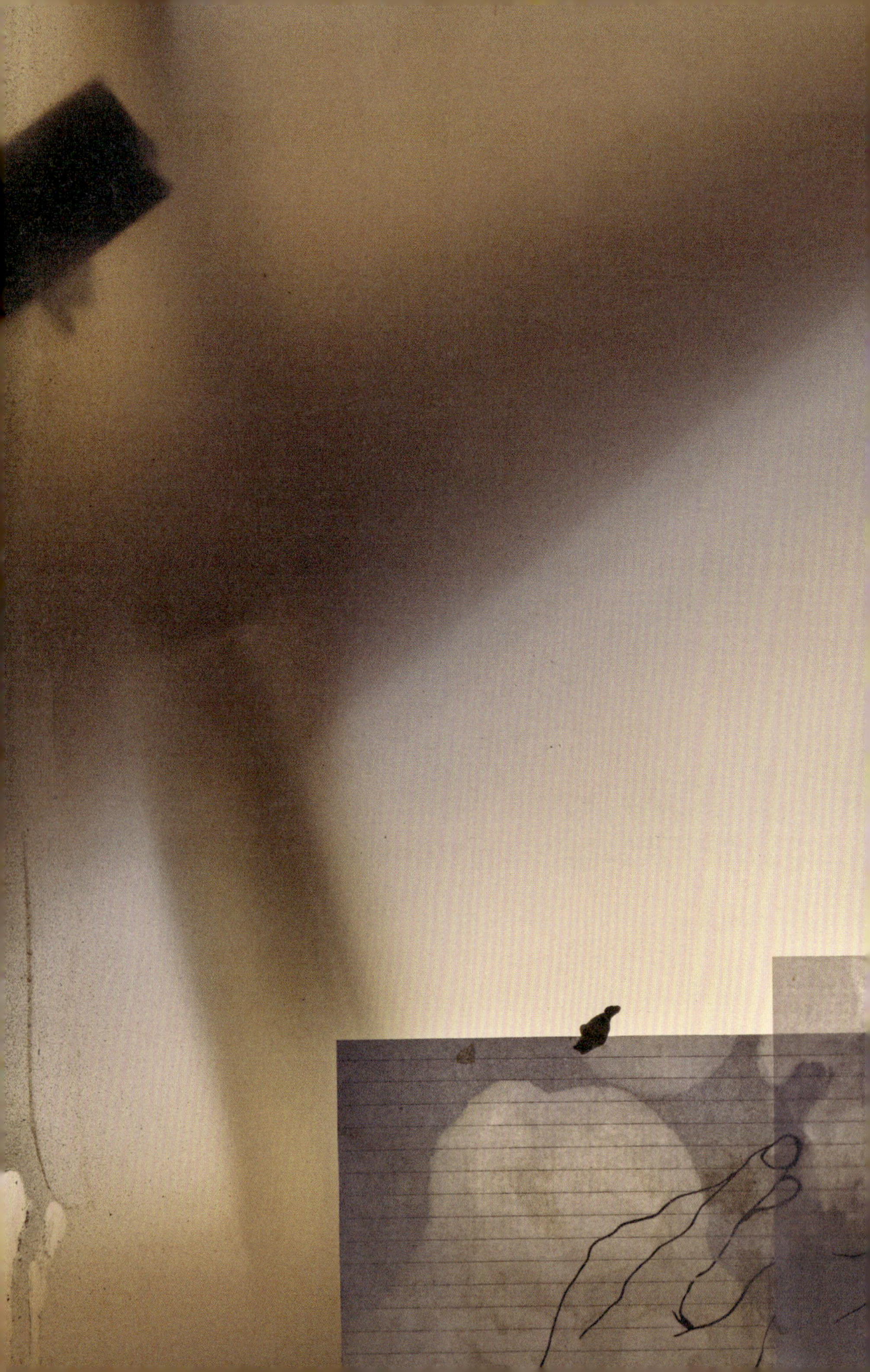

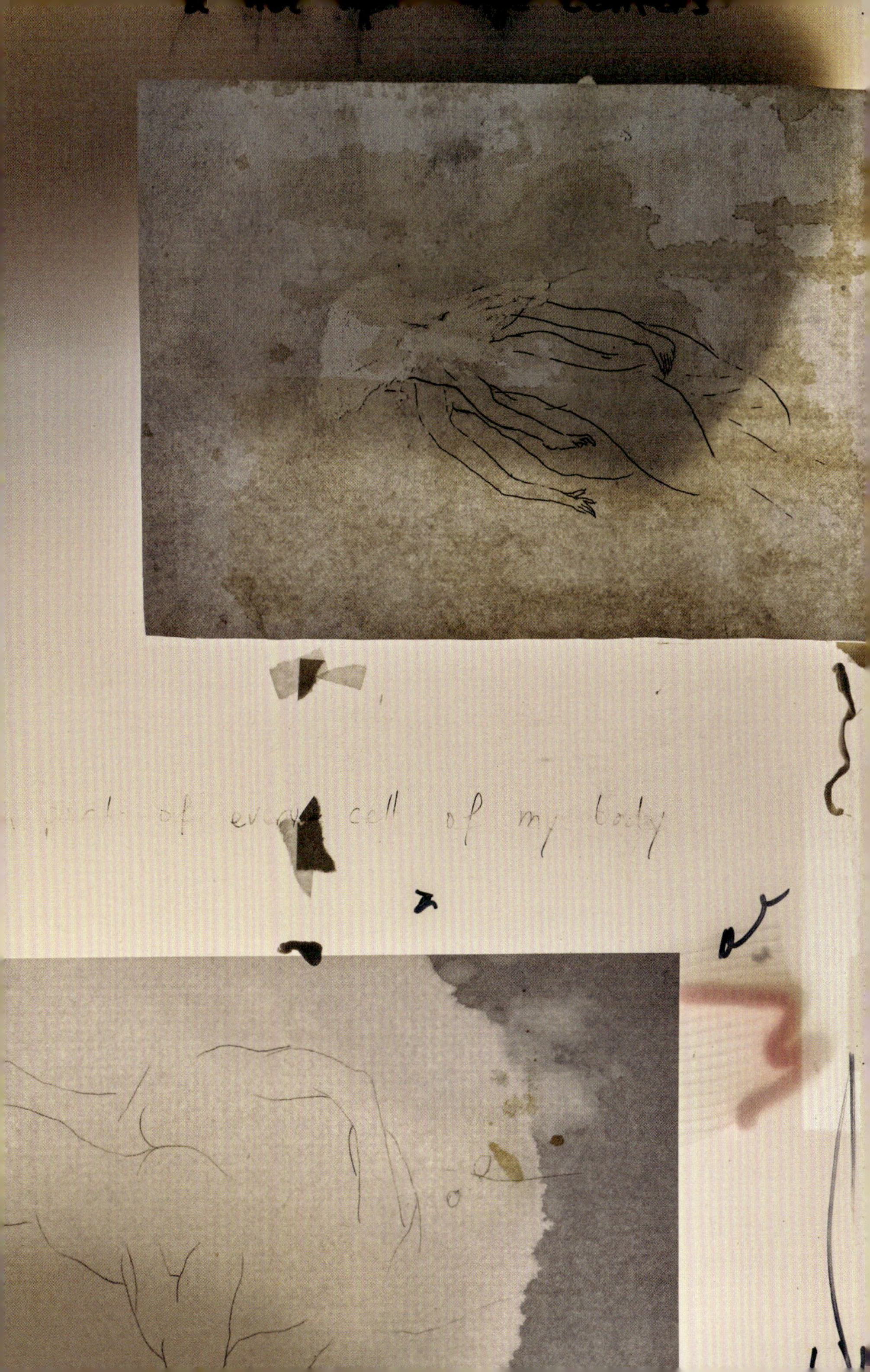
of every cell of my body

a list of strange

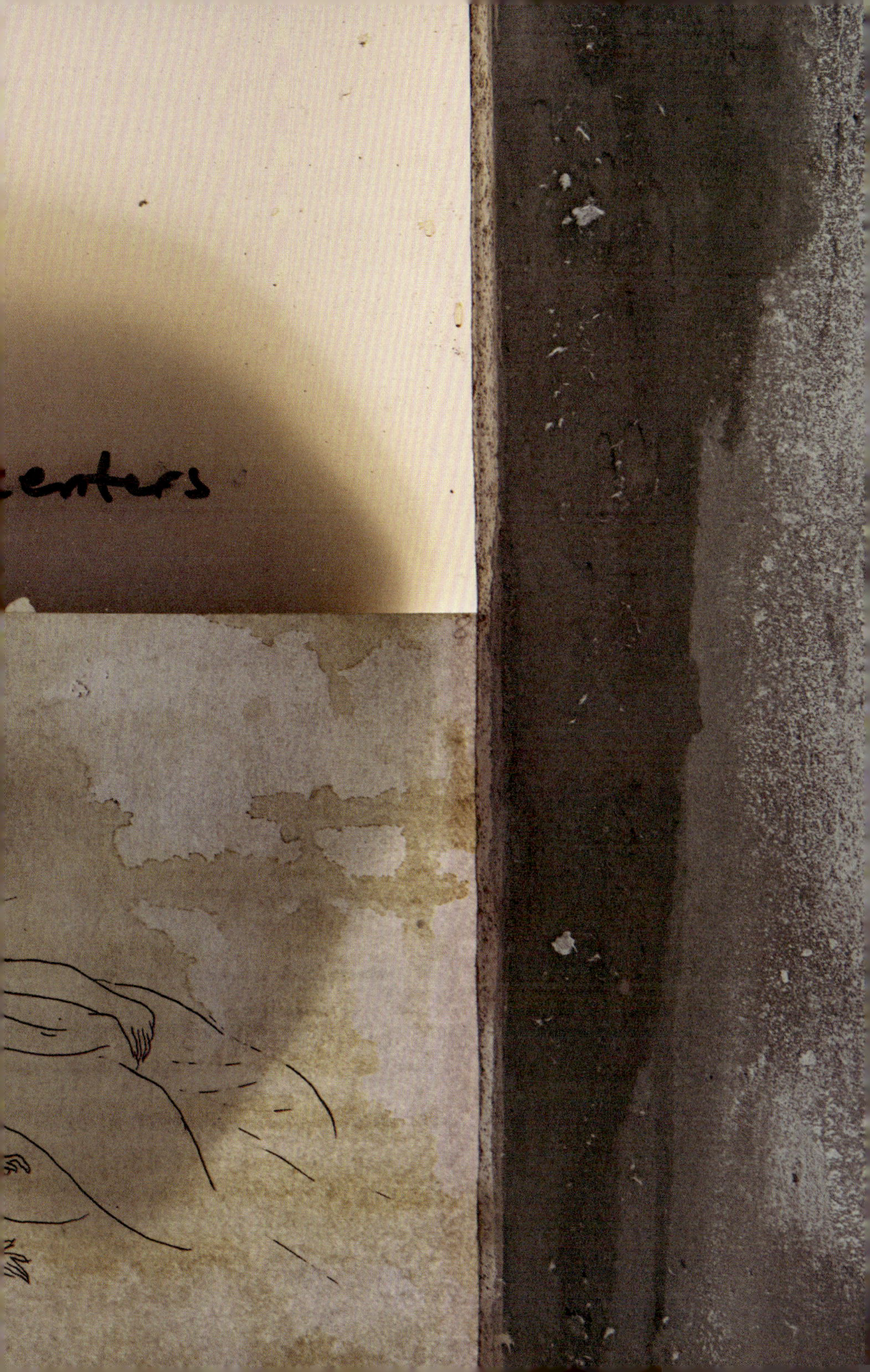
centers

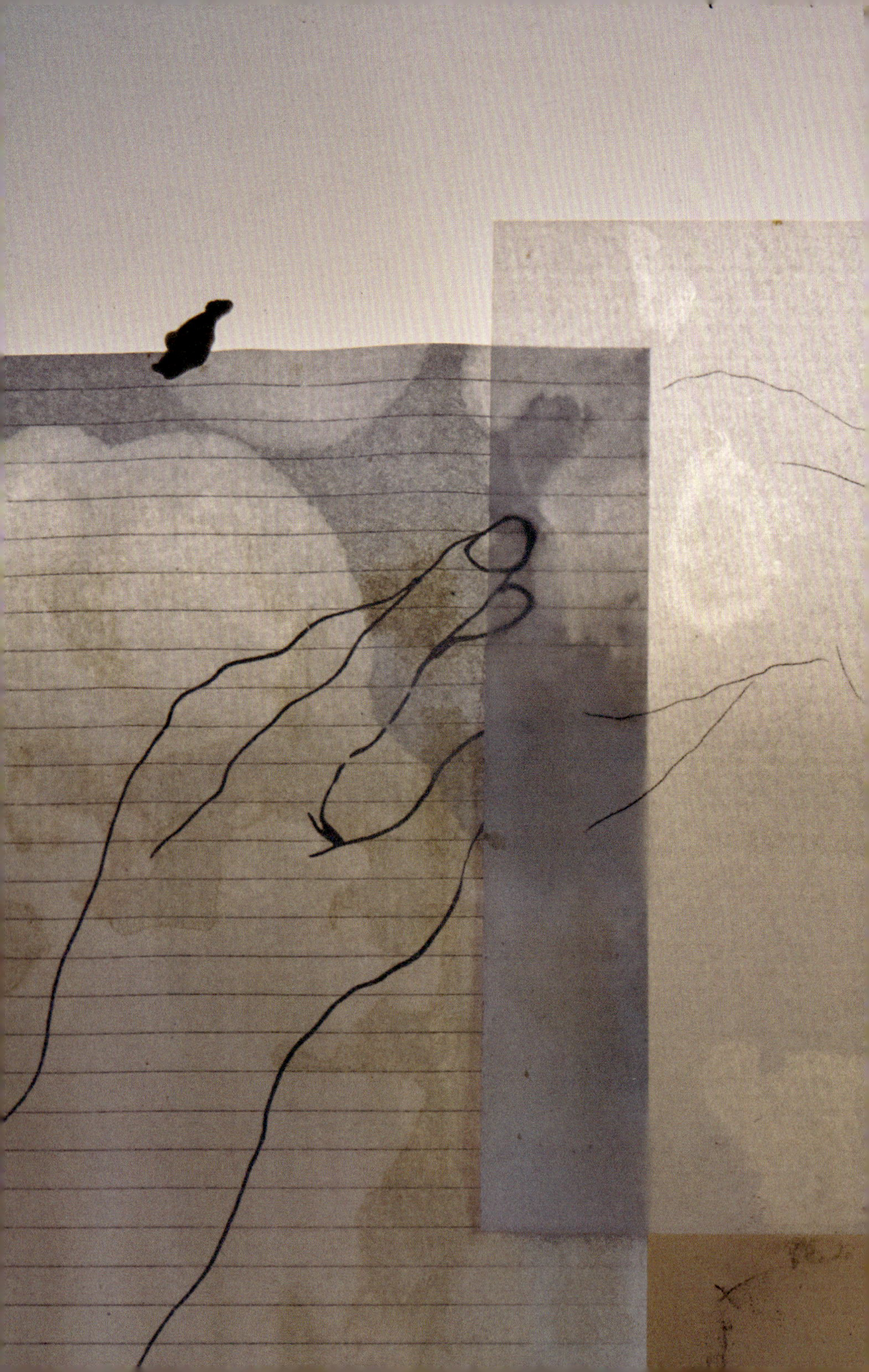

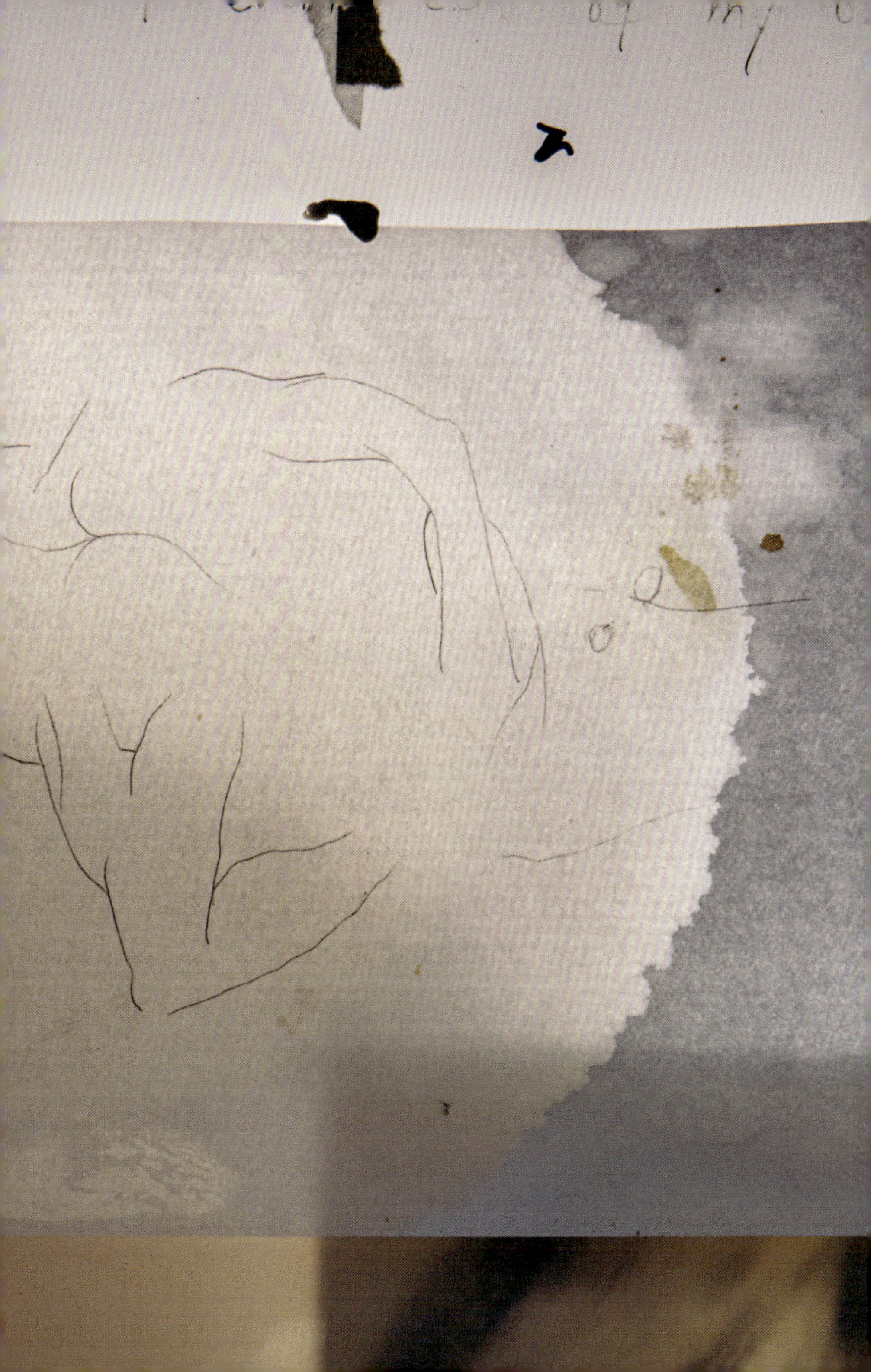

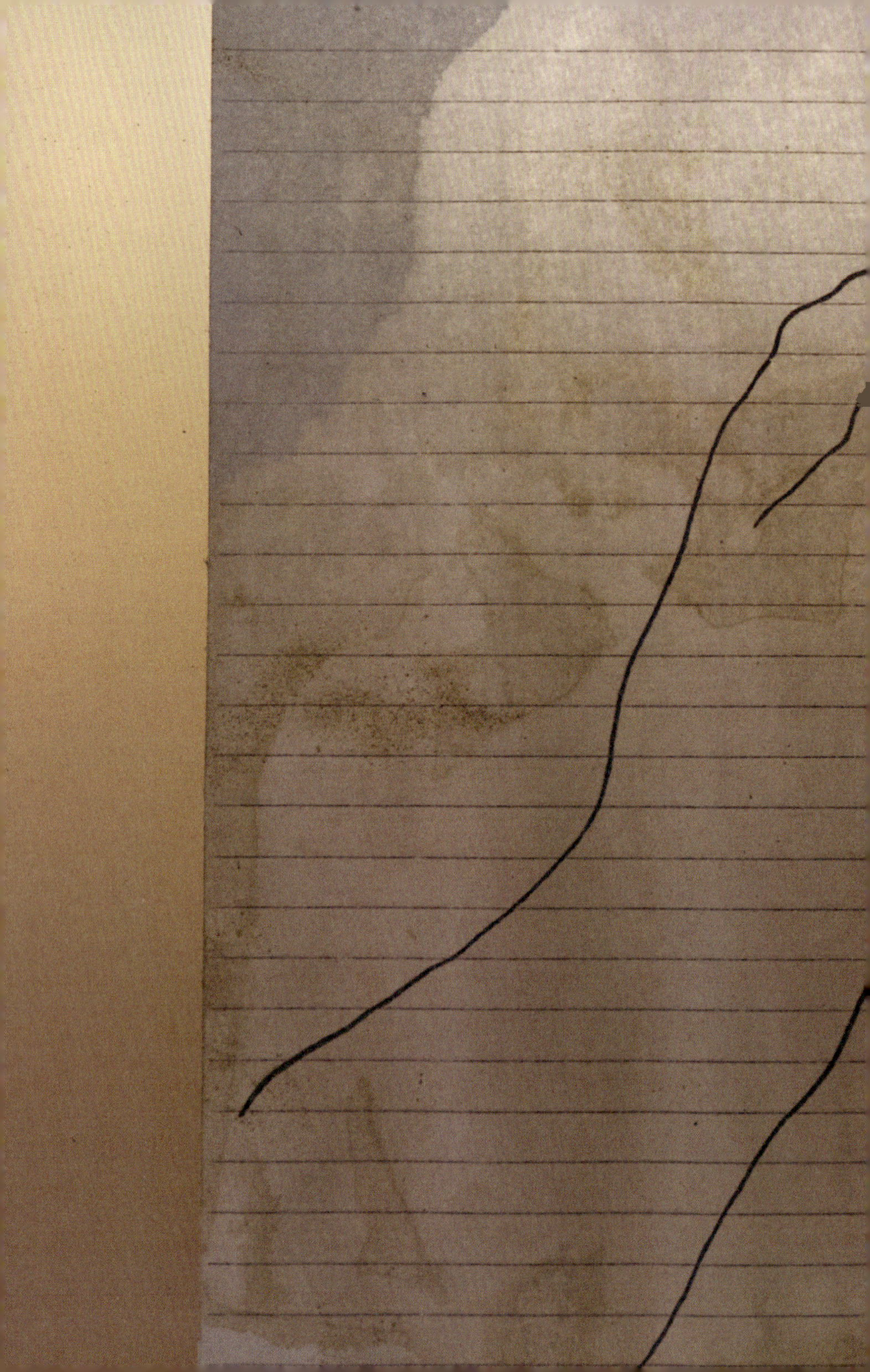

all was dark

A wound

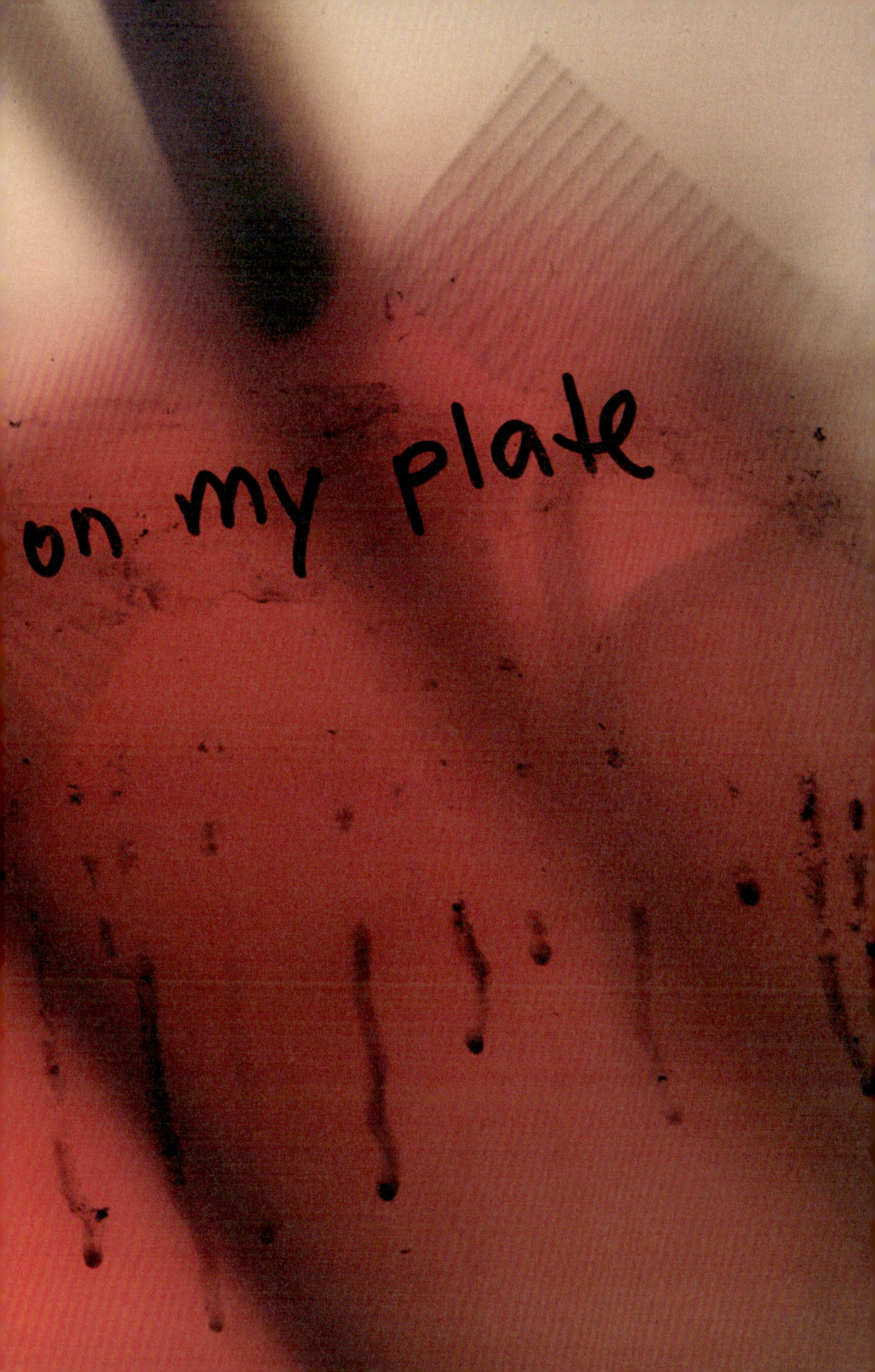
on my plate

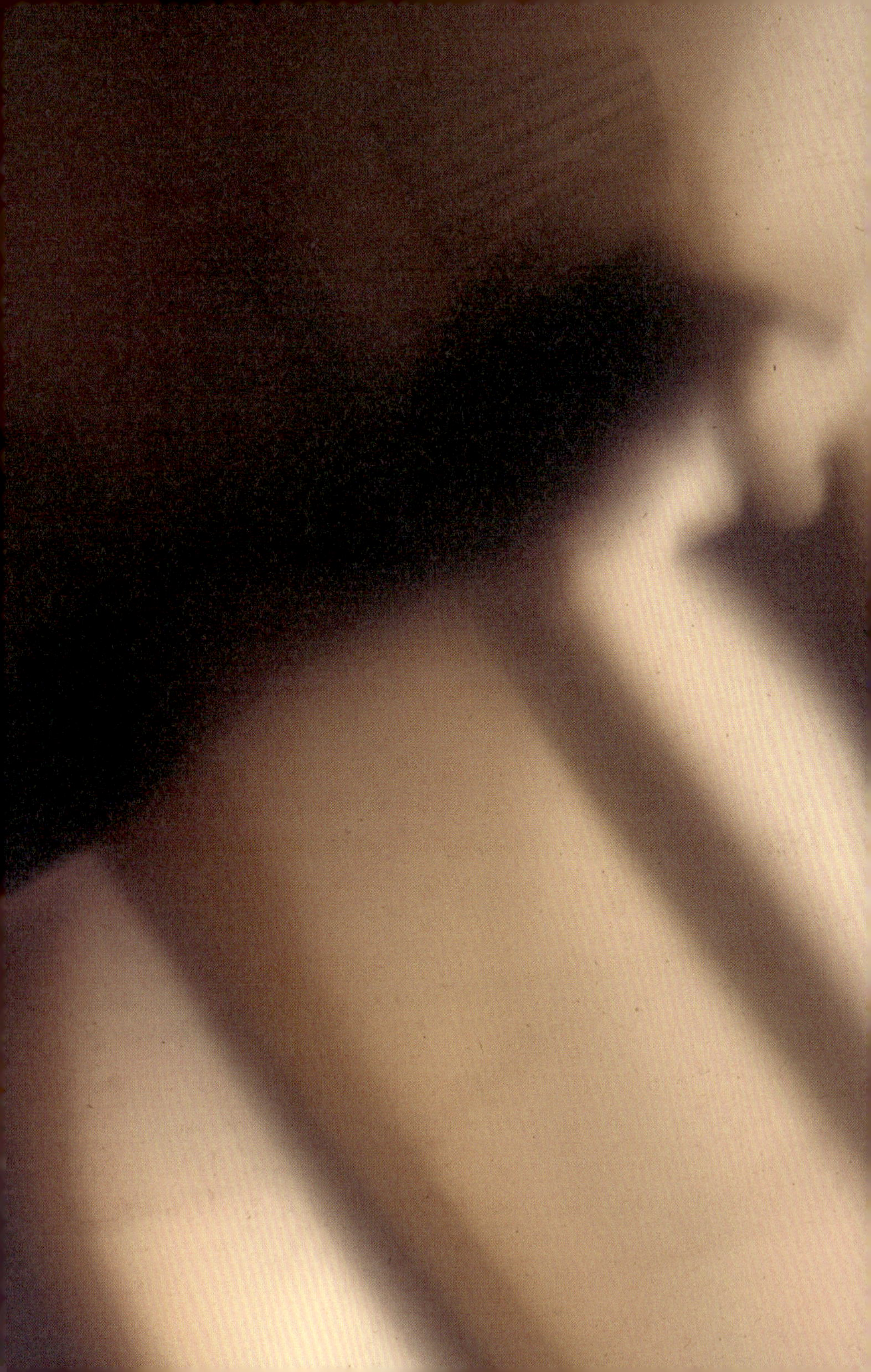

about expectations

hearly hardene

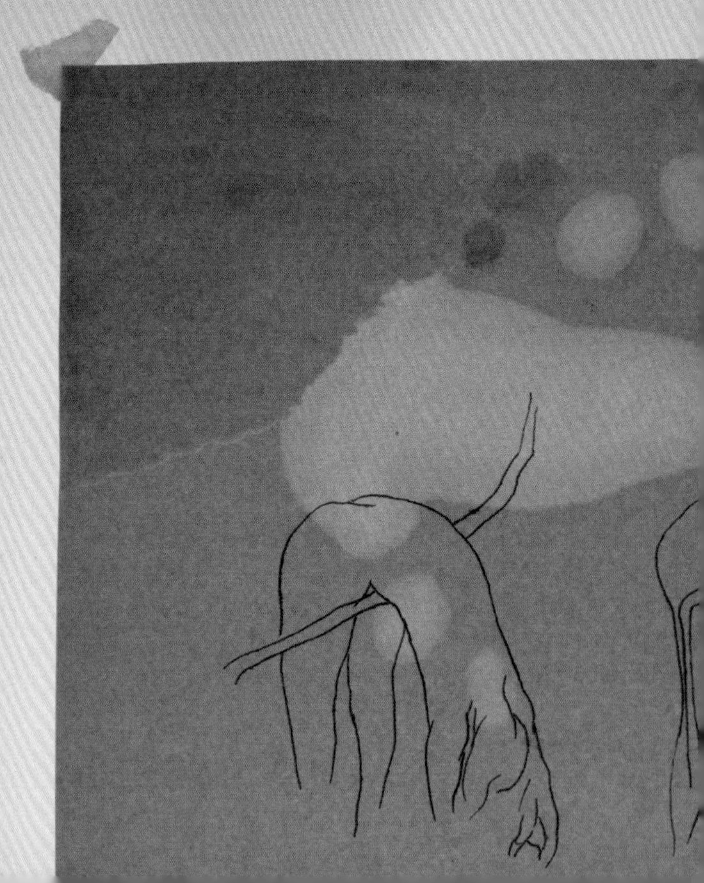

cold

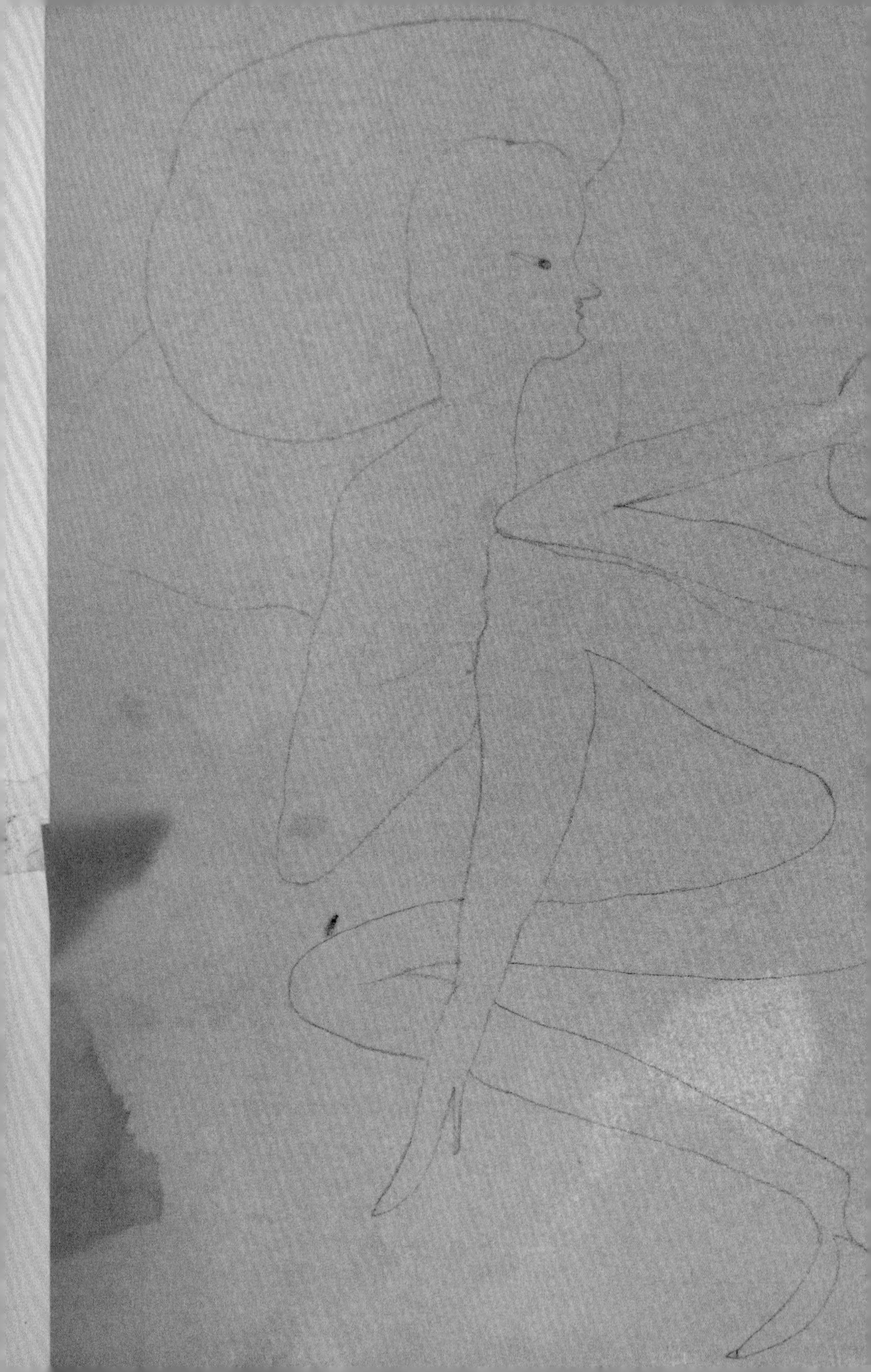

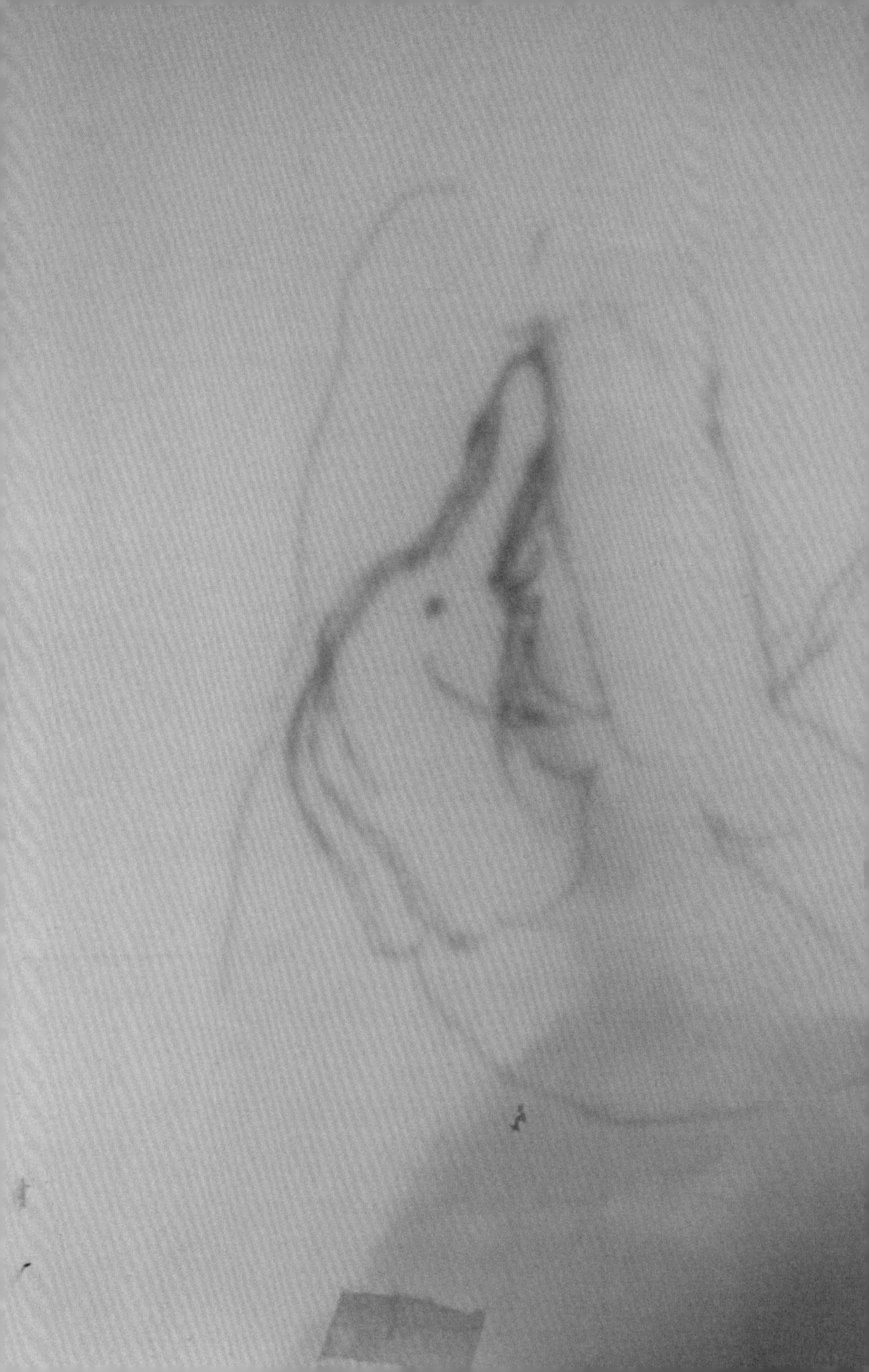

My chin was stuck on the opening. A self overlapping over self overlapping unto self. It is dark. I can not see but I sense the light is bright. I am warm and halfway outside.

Moments before this partial-exit, curled up inside, grasping the umbilical cord tightly, I said "Will you go?" Nothing happened.

Nothing happened. The pronunciation of the thing, the envisioning of the thing, never amounts to the thing itself. No need to fulfill—the beginning and end of my logic. Picture it all caving in, then picture building back up again. Opening your eyes afterwards, how to tell it hasn't happened?

It was this ineffectual verb—"go"—that solidified my non-pursuit. The decision was final: she would only wear dresses from this point forward—pants not fitting the determined "us."

In the room of the maternity unit, as she believed a future as "separate," I refused all efforts by physicians. Their arms reaching in: just another nested-within, the that-in-it, the multiply-present.

Despite excitement to see that fresh-made face slip out, Mother is haunted by the day Baby says (from a distance): You will grow old and I, your kid, will ignore you. I won't watch as you wither. As you look on, I won't be near to be seen surviving you. With inaction, nothing like "far" could happen now.

My persistence here has only just started, I say in the form of goo-goo-s and ga-ga-s. Though I seek to save you from missing me, you will be pilfered from my constancy: more goo-s and ga-s.

Here in the place before language arrived—while I still squirmed about legless and tethered—it had been just hum and drone. The hummmm and droooone was the matter of speech, not the filter nor form. From beyond the musculature of her lining, I could hear. Now—though I move across the land with toes outstretching—every word still must pass through this private sea to reach me.

So, it was an incomplete breech. I couldn't—no, wouldn't—get out. Yet, with legs touching the ground, I ran. She followed. The Mother body, like a ski-mask or hat drawn too far down over the ears eyes nose mouth. Her legs dangle down the sides of my yet-to-mature breasts.

I press against gravity, the force doctors believed would do the coaxing. I knew otherwise. A hand it played though—with rapid speed my limbs lengthened. Mere hours had passed until my toes touched the ground. By the first night, I outgrew the space from her pelvis to the floor. And then, as I learned to step one foot in front of the other, her soles hovered off the ground. Crumbs and dust grazed under her toes.

The word "person," null when settled in singular tense. Why lead life searching, when I could choose to never let go what I already have? In this place we share called "world," it is not a good fit as it once was. Thrust out of a perfect pairing, and landing ... where? Determined I was not to find myself in similar fate. And, without much transformation at all, the magnetic child I endured to be.

It is a short life for me. Compressed—years in the span of hours.

Our sharing of blood overtakes us. If in construction, I am half Mother half Father, to be a joined thing between her, then she is ... like three-fourths of an individual, yes? Funny thing, being double the person and still not even yourself.

And me—in my obstinance—never knowing my own face, it remaining beneath the blanket of her body. Hers was a beautiful one, seen by me after the procedure. (Whereby the doctors—who are so nice—create small incisions for my eyeballs). She would bend down and I would look at her looking at me—albeit upside down.

Just as we would come to pass, the lines on her forehead and beneath her eyes quickly deepened. I have not the signs of age, remaining immature, rejuvenated by fluids of progesterone—amniotic. The human has been shaped by mechanical demands for feeding, and of that I had unorthodox method. She was my channel. Why the need for mouth? Why the need for teeth? Why the need for throat or even stomach? The nutrients came as it had—solid, through her to sludge, transfixed to me, absorbed.

My facial muscles, in their pubescent fervor, graft and weft with Mother. Any attempt at severing would leave her without abdomen. She would become just a neck, and then wither towards death. In perpetuity, this—my helmet of meat within hermetic sealing.

Her face dragged across the ceiling from our maladaptation to architecture. Buildings just aren't made for two. I continued to grow, and she continued to sand down.

I wake up one day in our bed, and the drapes look different. I go to lift myself out of bed, but Mother doesn't awake with me. I lay nearly trapped, fixed sweaty back to sheets. The top-heavy weightfulness: She does not budge. Past the stomach acid that coats my ears, I make out her maintaining unceasing snoring.

I manage not to stand upright, but it is enough to crawl. Today is a day, just like others, and I won't allow her to keep me bedridden over some laziness. The coffeepot—which I can't reach from the floor—is already brewing, is someone here?

I move along quietly as can be. Inspecting corners, closets, and beneath furniture. Despite everything slightly ajar, nothing in the house breathes beside her and I. Well, okay, just the wrong side of bed today I suppose, nothing more. Then, going back into our bedroom, I see on the floor a note. It is from her.

“I won’t live like this anymore, to be in your wake every moment. We will, from this day forward, be out of sync. While you sleep, I will live, vice versa. I am sorry for any confusion, but my decision is firm. The logistics we will figure out in time. As we adapted, we will again. Please do not fight me on this.”

Betraying our difficult symbiosis, our body ached and creaked, the weight of the other—carried and dragged. I never hear her voice anymore. She never hears mine. I’d turn her body—its limpness—to look at her, but her breath reeks stale and of sleep. During her hours, does she pretend I’m gone or does she peer down at my body—its limpness? I needed to imagine she hadn’t left me so. Relay me the weekend movie. At very least. Tell me how you slept. Caress me gently.

I still take us to the park and imagine her laughing like she would as she touched the doggy ears. It felt like talking to stone and imagining it lives.

Throughout my outbursts with which I'd awake her, she wondered: ... to inflict that which will not mirror to me? She couldn't lock me in the bathroom. No knees on rice. No counting backwards from one million (that monotonous toil would bore her to death). "It hurts me to hurt you." My neck and her opening a horizon of terror not exempt from itself, nor flipping.

I did not share her lactose intolerance—which, I'll put plainly: became her mechanism of punishment.

After-pause ...*the-worthy-millionsexclamation-honest-manner-living-this-accidents-comes-from-evil-tired-unbearable-connected-sinking-fainting-depths*. She'd shat all down my back.

These new days "alone" passed with slowness. The light shone on the walls of the house. Shelving had been installed three-quarters up the wall, holding duplicates of every object that I would grab from scatterings below. Through all this stuff of life paired, I could trace her waking hours after the fact.

I took to extended naps throughout the day, to join her company. Without her cooking, my meals were skipped. I grew thinner. My interests faded. I would let the television channel she was watching as she went to sleep continue playing.

I missed when we had settled for our we-ness. Walking about as I was, this reminder of my cruelty trailing. A voice inside said: Cut her loose. Cut who loose? There is no "her" and no "I." This voice clearly knows nothing—that body up top is me. I would respond saying "Would you cut yourself in half?!"

My reason lives in a house with my doubting. The perhaps, the should-have, the better-if, the may-be-had, all dining together. Unusual comedy mounting to sublime effect, I began to see that word (I) could never quite refer correctly—the (I) which had been turned to (we) eternally settled in as a forever-thing.

The massiveness of that word: "eternally"... It sat as a boulder before me, us. I tried to break fate into smaller moments, thinking that maybe then it would be easier. No rain came down. No waves crashed inward. No strong man quite strong enough—to splice the stone to sand.

We dream: The sun is out. Green cast hovers atop everything, it must be spring. The image in front bobs up and down, like the whole world sat on a raft floating on turbulent tides, or like someone incessantly nodding their head in agreement. It is my little girl's birthday. There is a cake and she is clapping. I want to see her, this is all I can think. What does she look like? What might she look like beneath all of me?

Everything keeps kinetic. Stabilizing my sight is futile so I give up, allowing everything to move. Only here do I start to grasp the fervent horizon. I see hair—wet, foamy, pink. Matted. No, this can't be—I think. The dizziness refuses to budge. Baby is looking around. I believe she is searching for me. This dream, this place, outside in spring, the light drowning down, the birds in the sky.

Here Daughter is a shining lovely sponge of life.

The image switches: I'm seeing through Daughter's eyes now, as she searches for, me. The gaze settles upon a canine licking again and again at its wound: wet, foamy, pink. Matted. Her with my eyes, hops down from the chair and waddles towards the mutt. It continues lapping itself, head bobbing up and down to further its tongue into the flaps of the gash. I realize why I've been seeing everything shake up and down. I am licking the wound. The whole thing is covered in fleas. And those fleas are covered in fleas. Covered in fleas.

It is a cold morning waking up. We are in bed, in the sliver of time where she falls into sleep and I out of it.

There is wet on the windowsill. Something feels good. Suddenly, somehow, without me sensing any signs the days prior. She starts to leave. I follow.

What if we called it sleep? What if we called it no-dream-land? What if we called it some nights? What if we called it half-state? With these final moments, each question contains the royal (we), the royal (I), the precious (we).

The letters of her name reconfigured like a puzzle. The meaning of "her," just as words like "me," or "together," all disintegrating into "further-from-the-contents-of-a-good-nothing." Everything wept out, the matter and otherwise. Remaining meant nān.

"Finally, self," she says with our last air. The bits that remain of her worn-down skull keel over, hitting the bedside, jerking my neck along with them. The chamber leaks. A viscose texture adding to the swarm of fluid, and I could tell the difference. I can tell the difference. Temperature. Taste. Acidity. I coughed again. This juice—which now made me understand our contrast all along—flooded upwards. Again. And then, I began to choke, to drown.

At the end of nowhere, my chin was stuck on the opening.

Jacksun Bein

At the end of nowhere, my chin was stuck on the opening.

Jacksun Bein

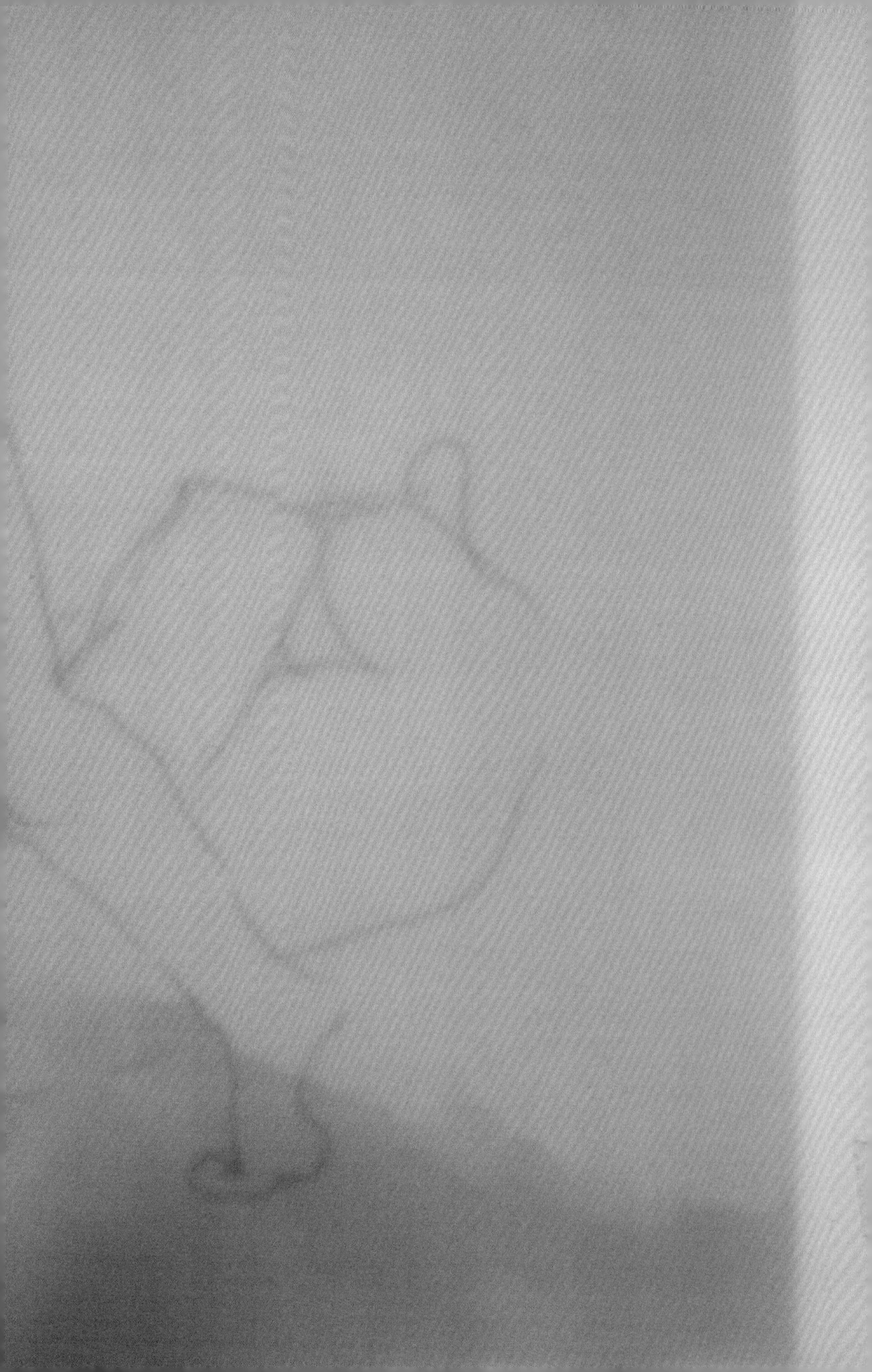

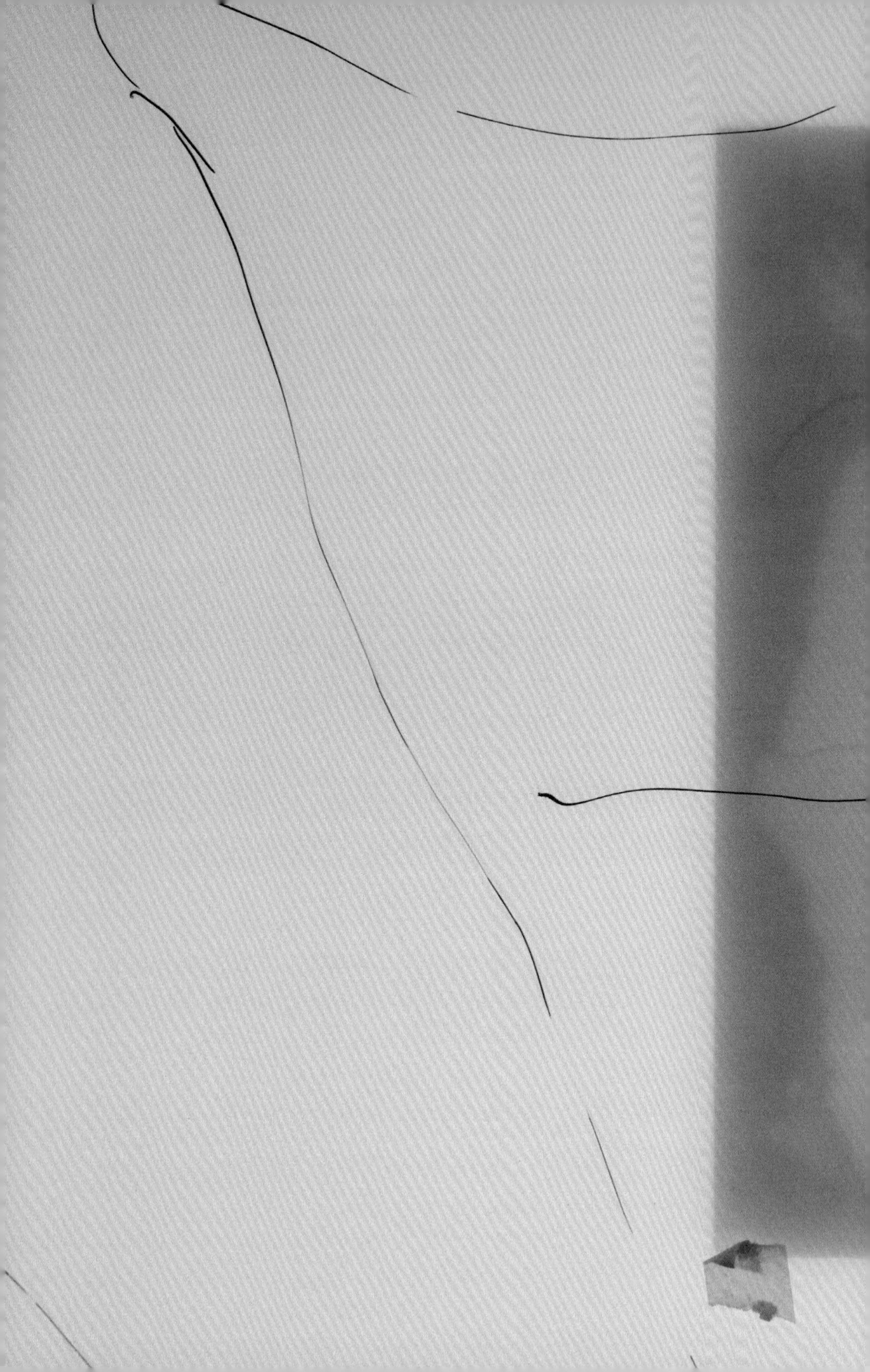

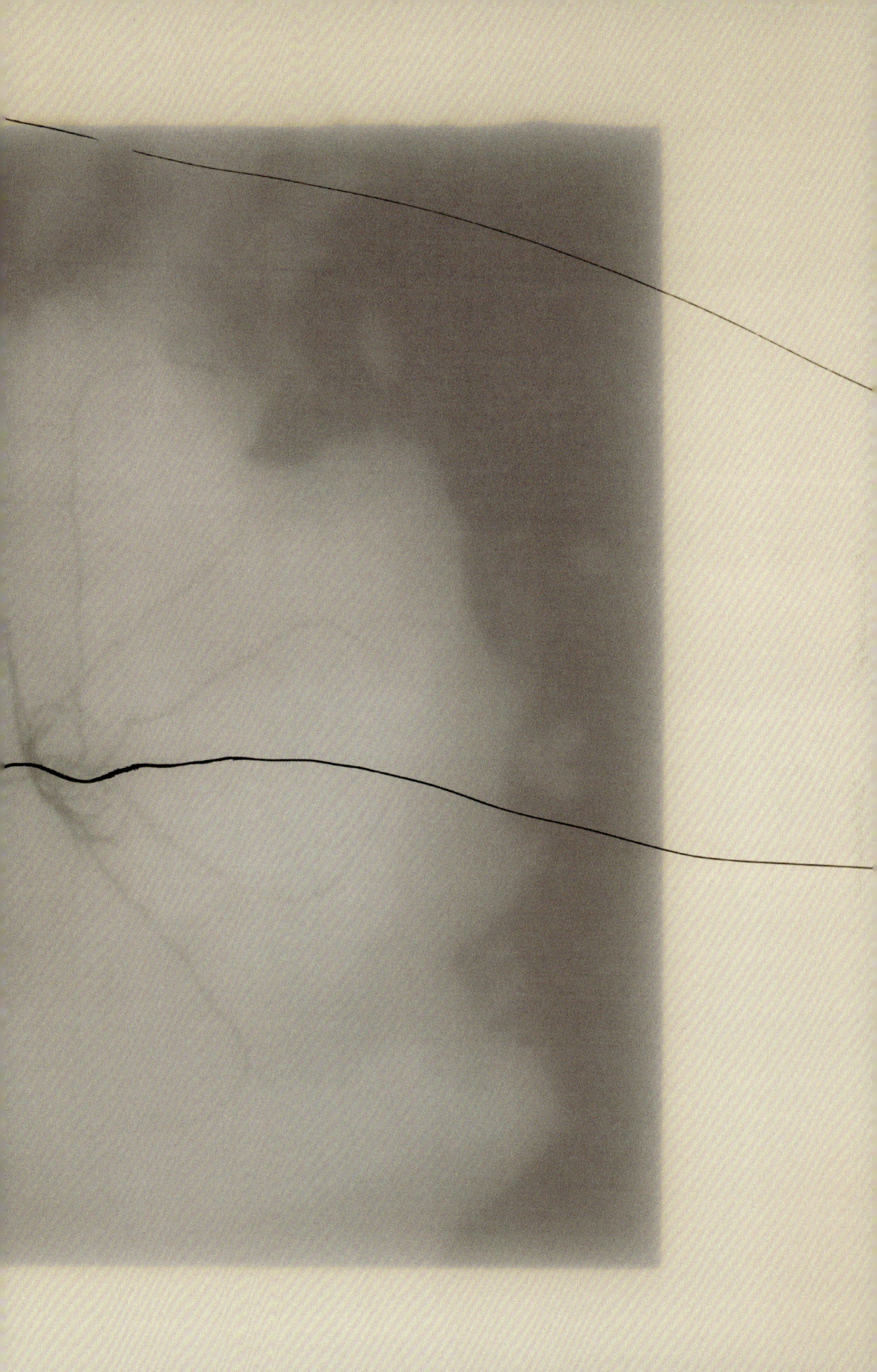

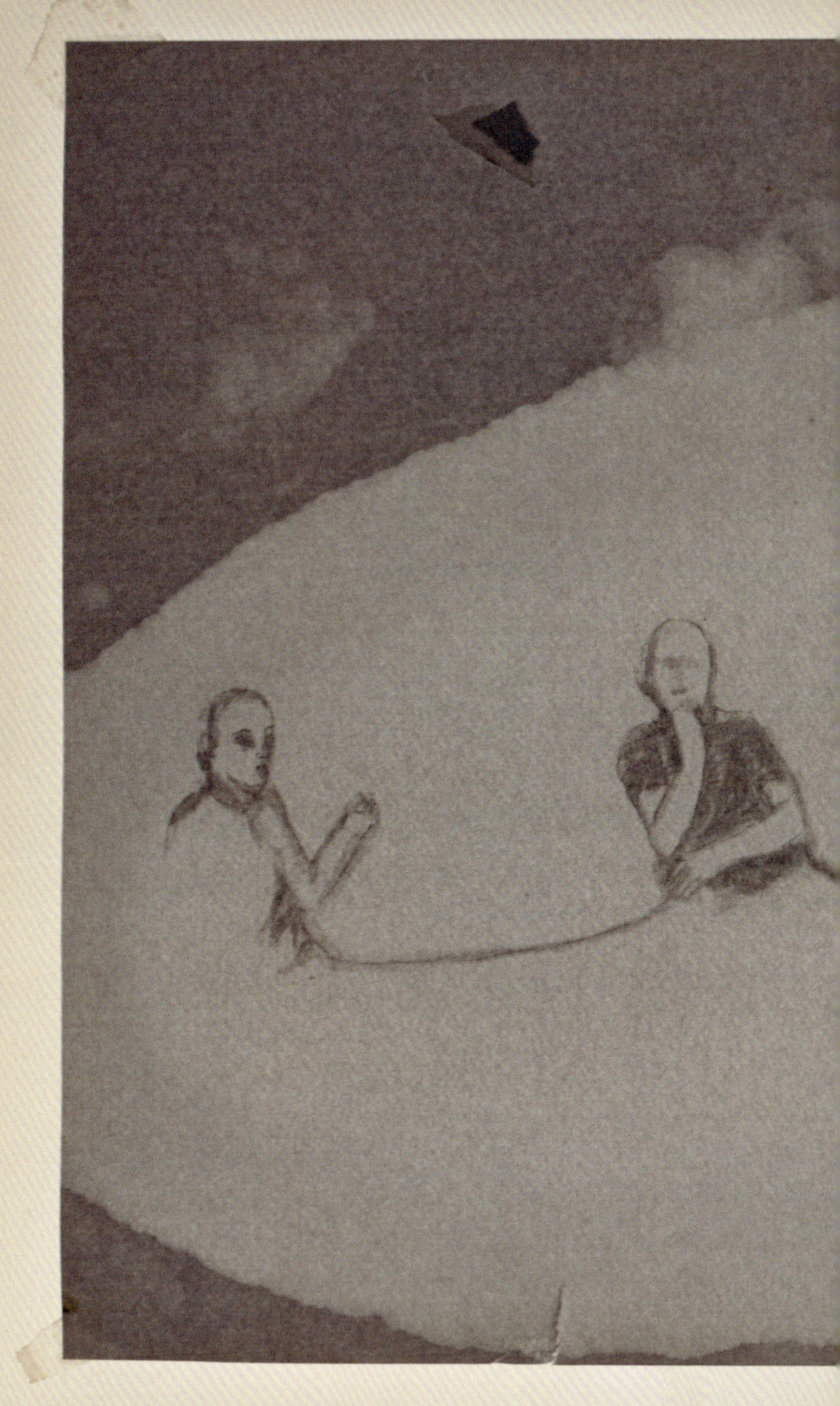

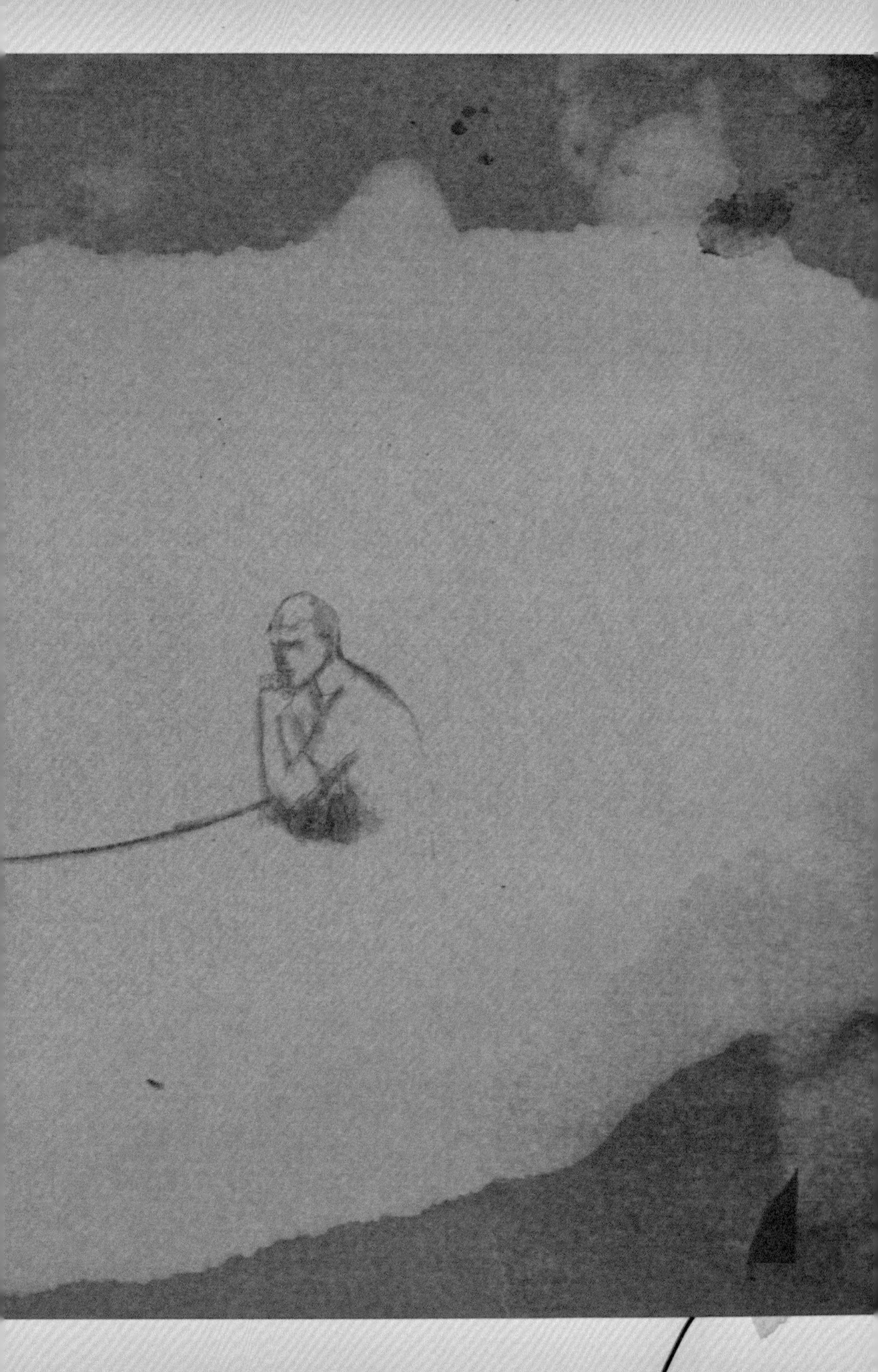

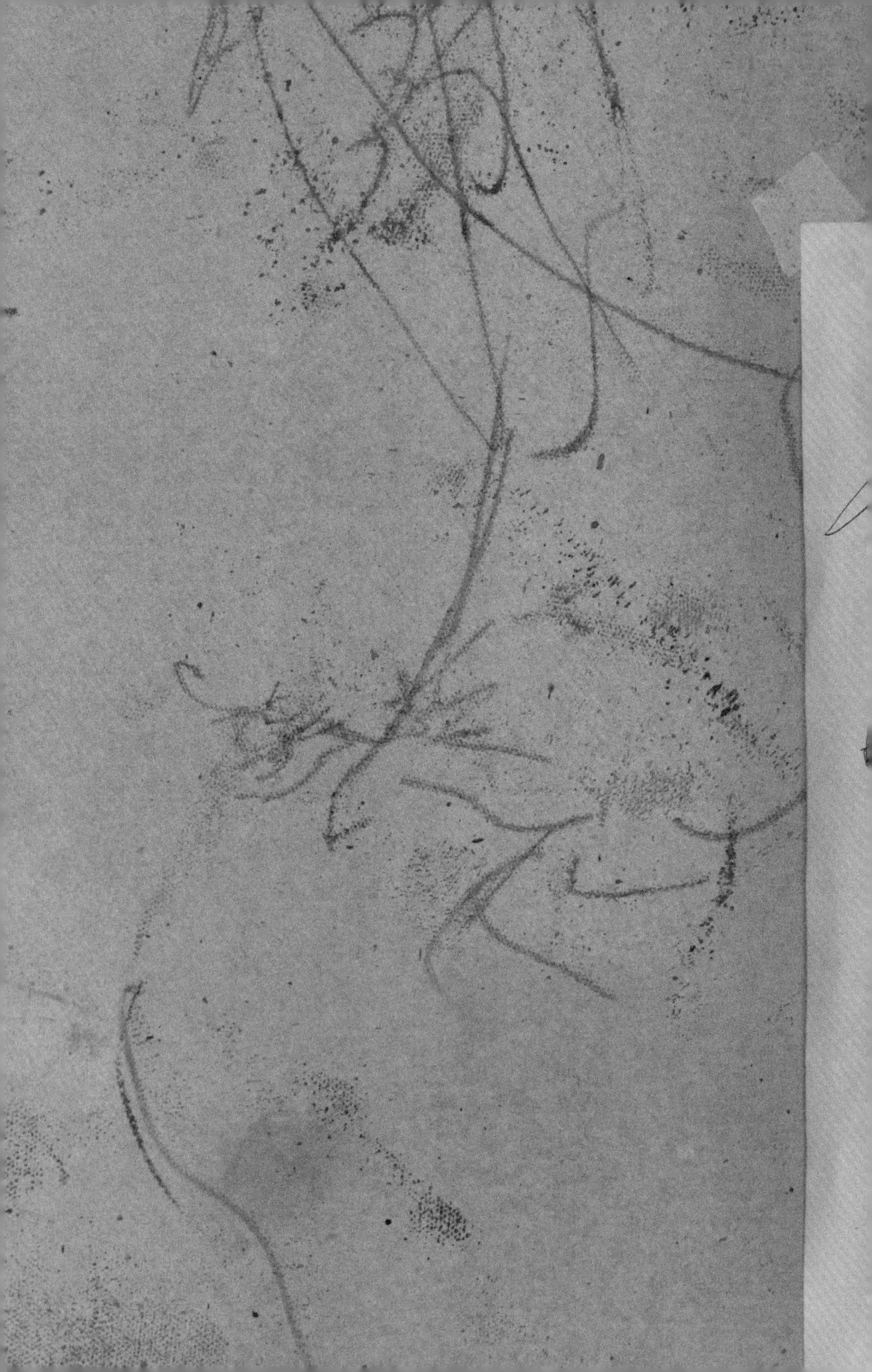

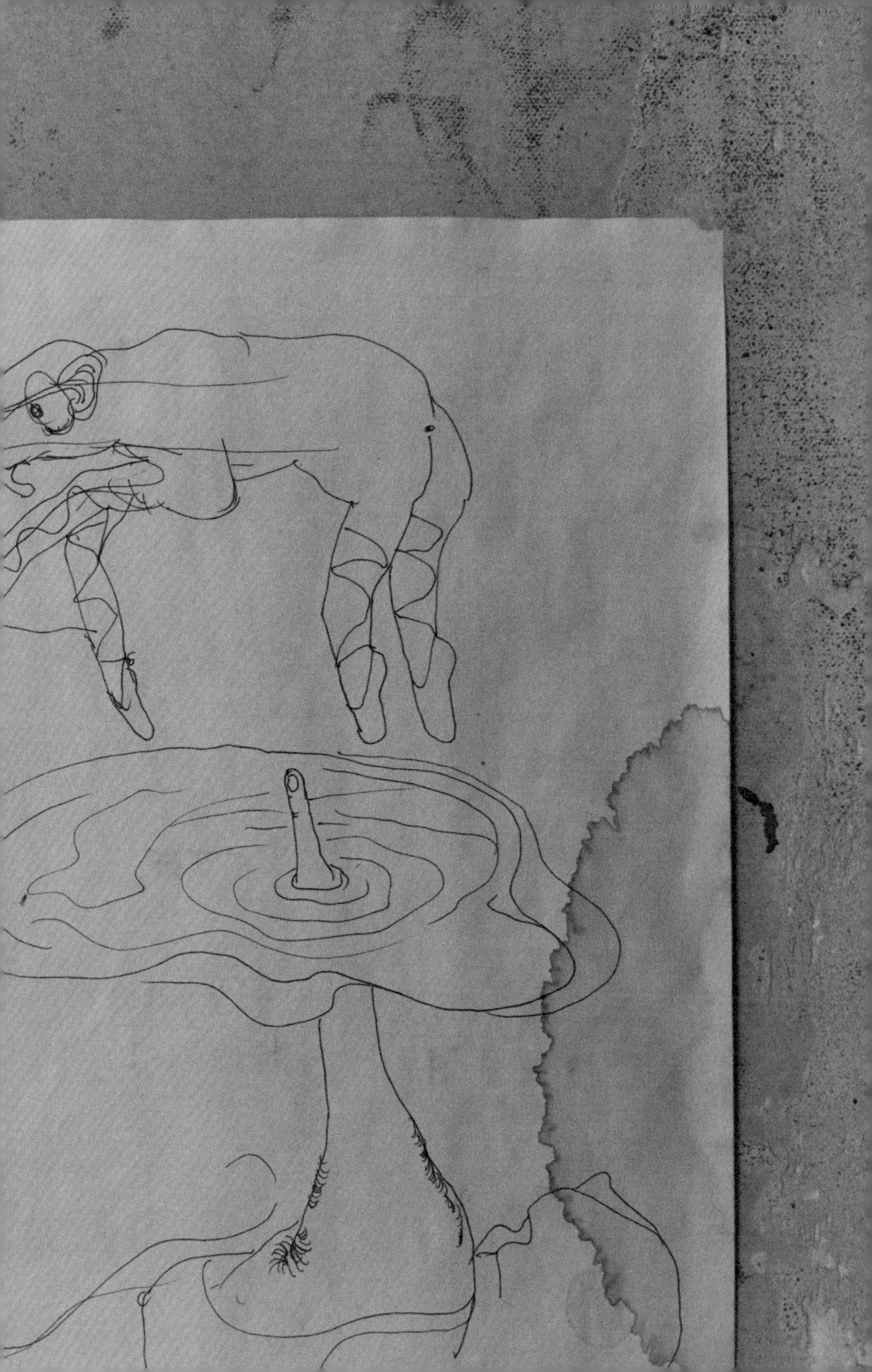

as if we have a great
time

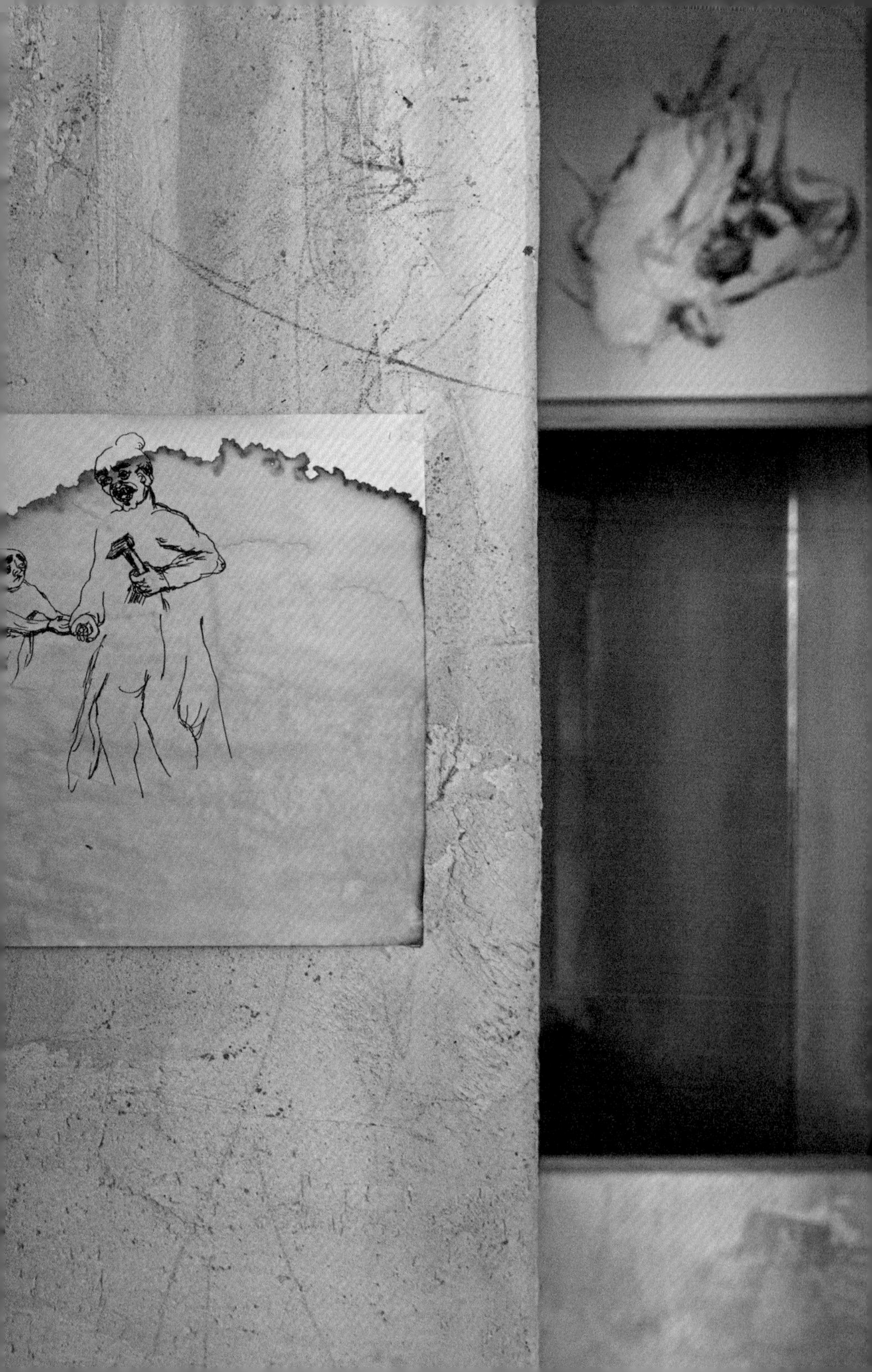

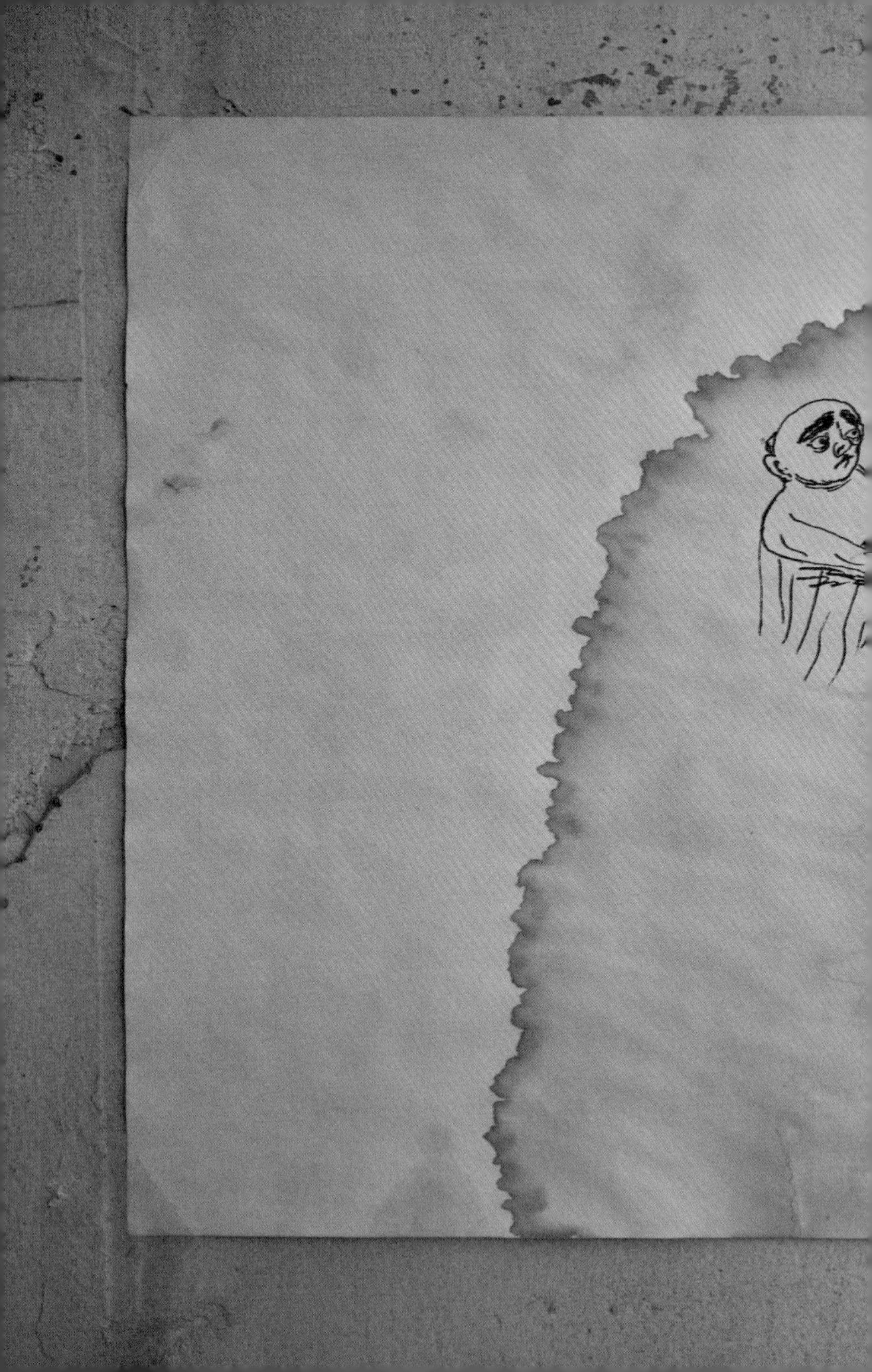

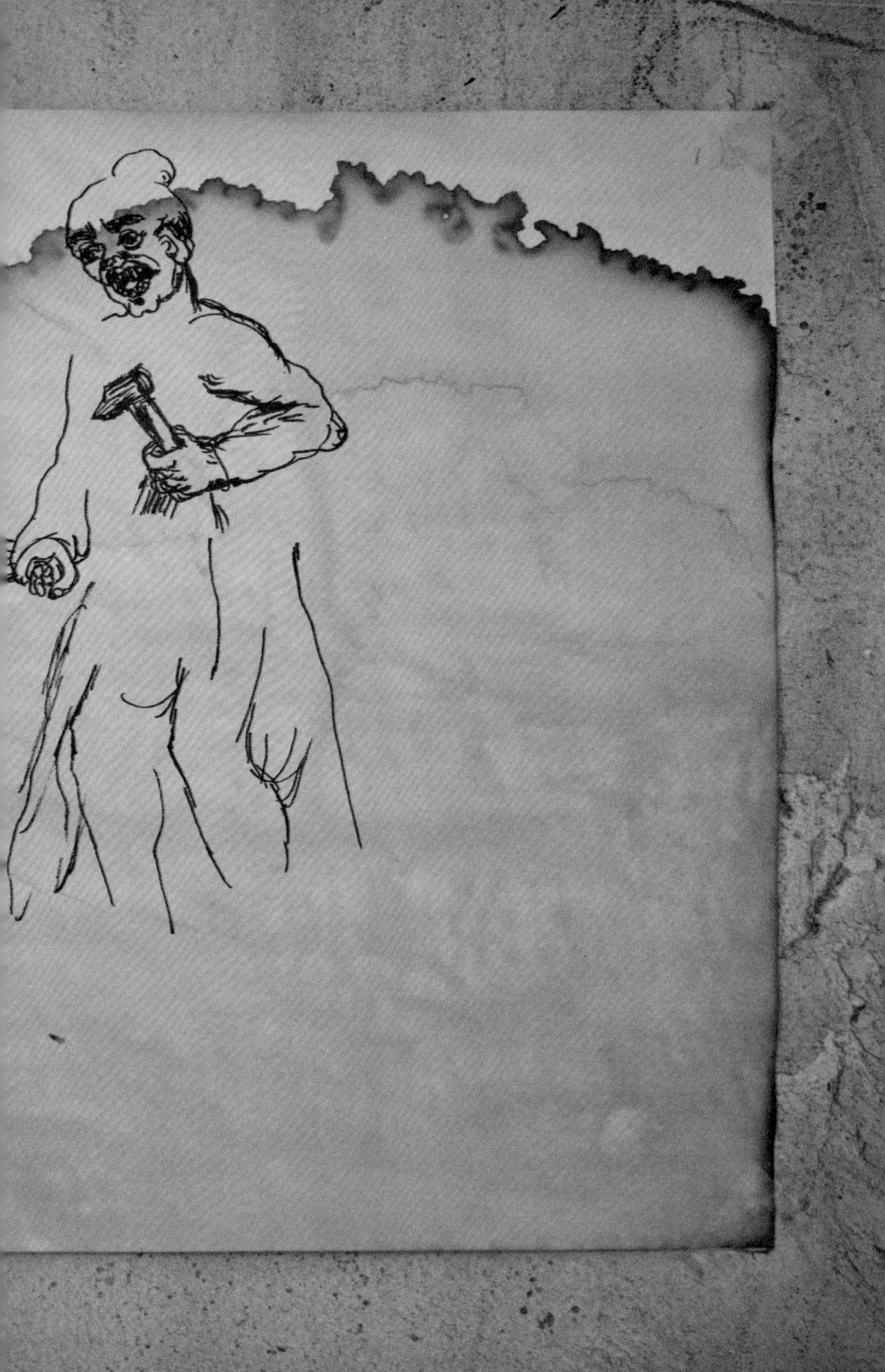

I like

it mak

saying Jac
me feel
cool

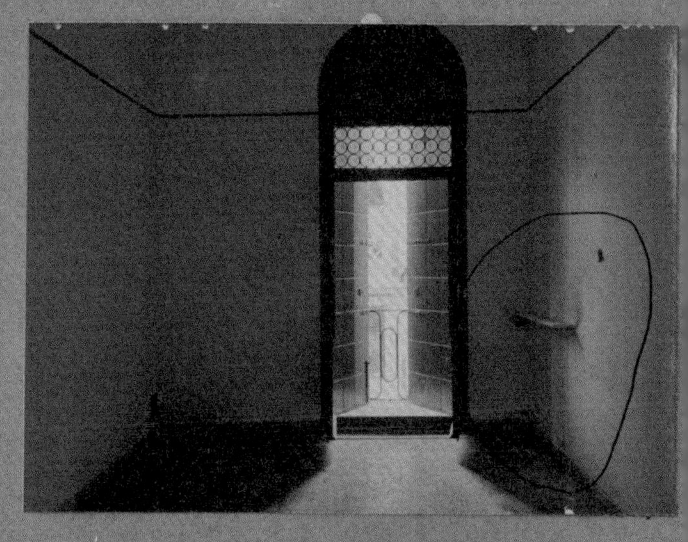

il nice when people stop and

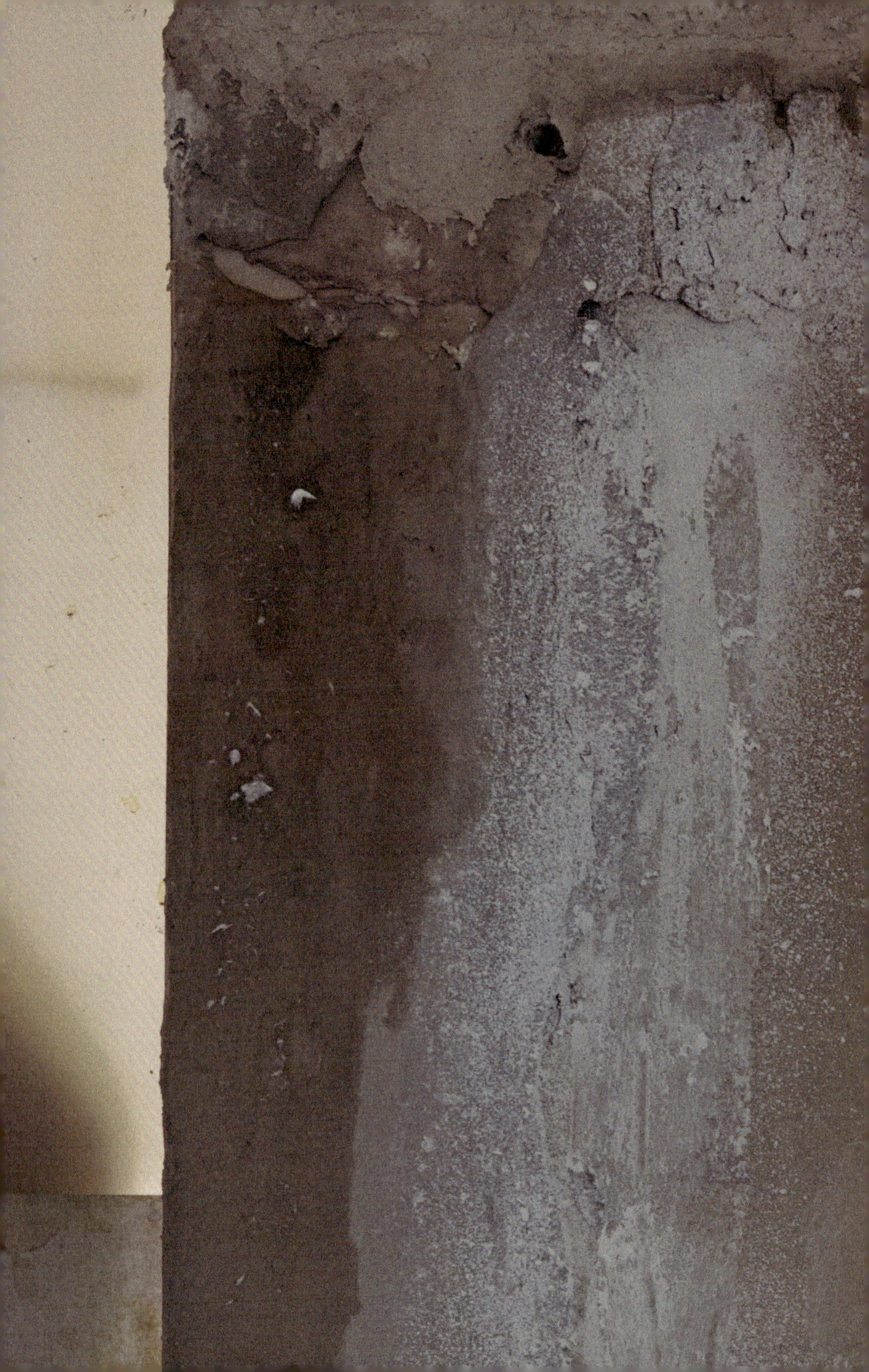

a close up of things

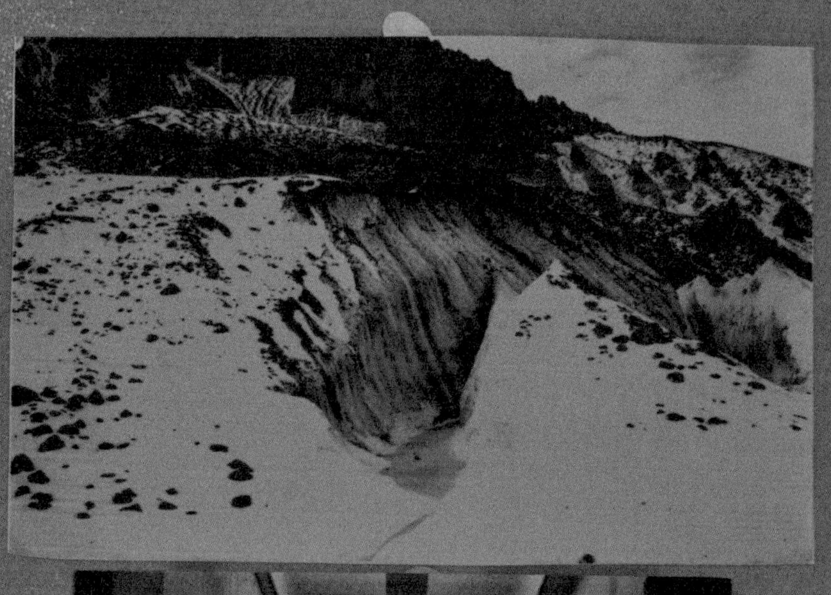

sk/m is not tra[illegible]
enough

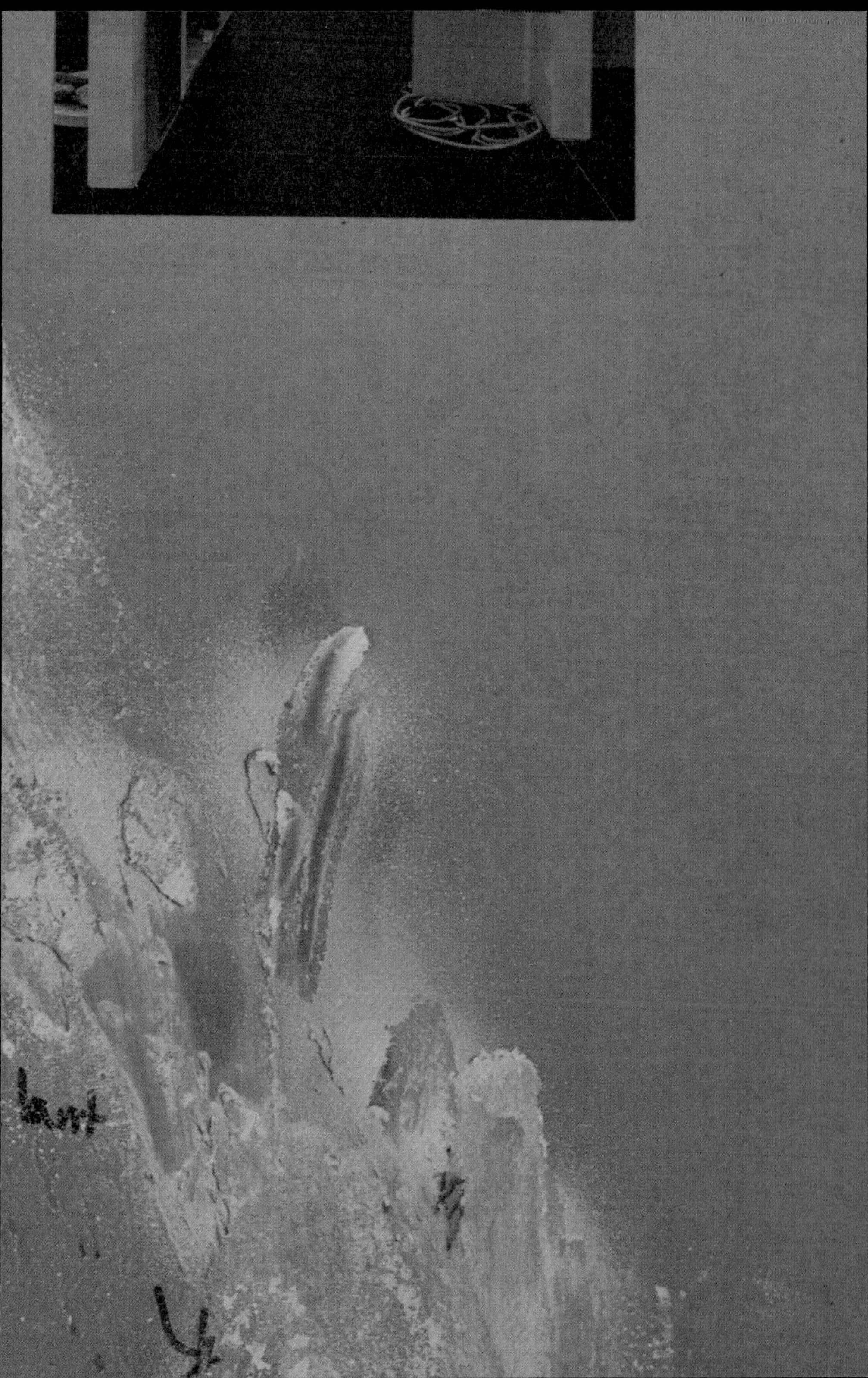

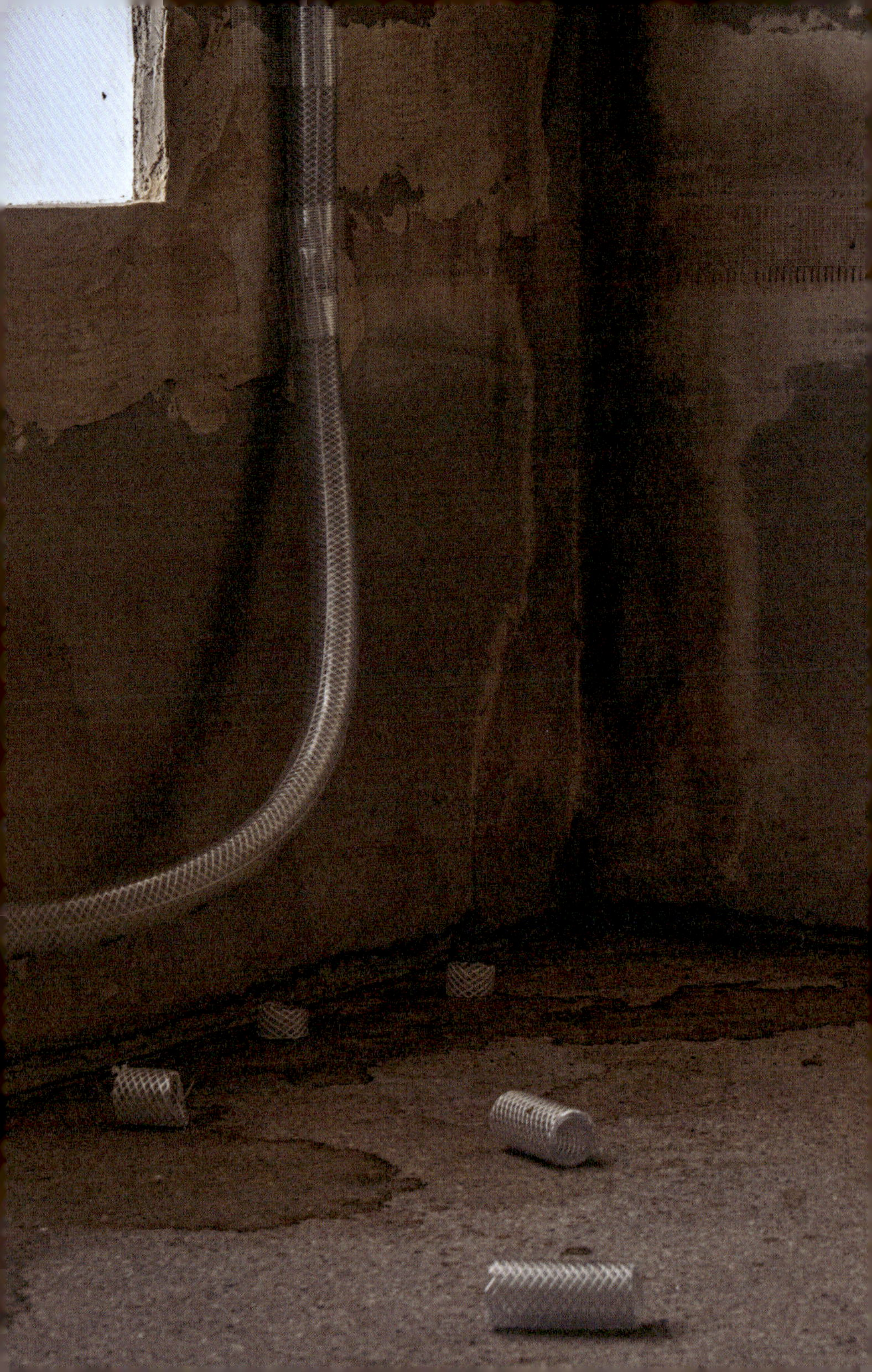

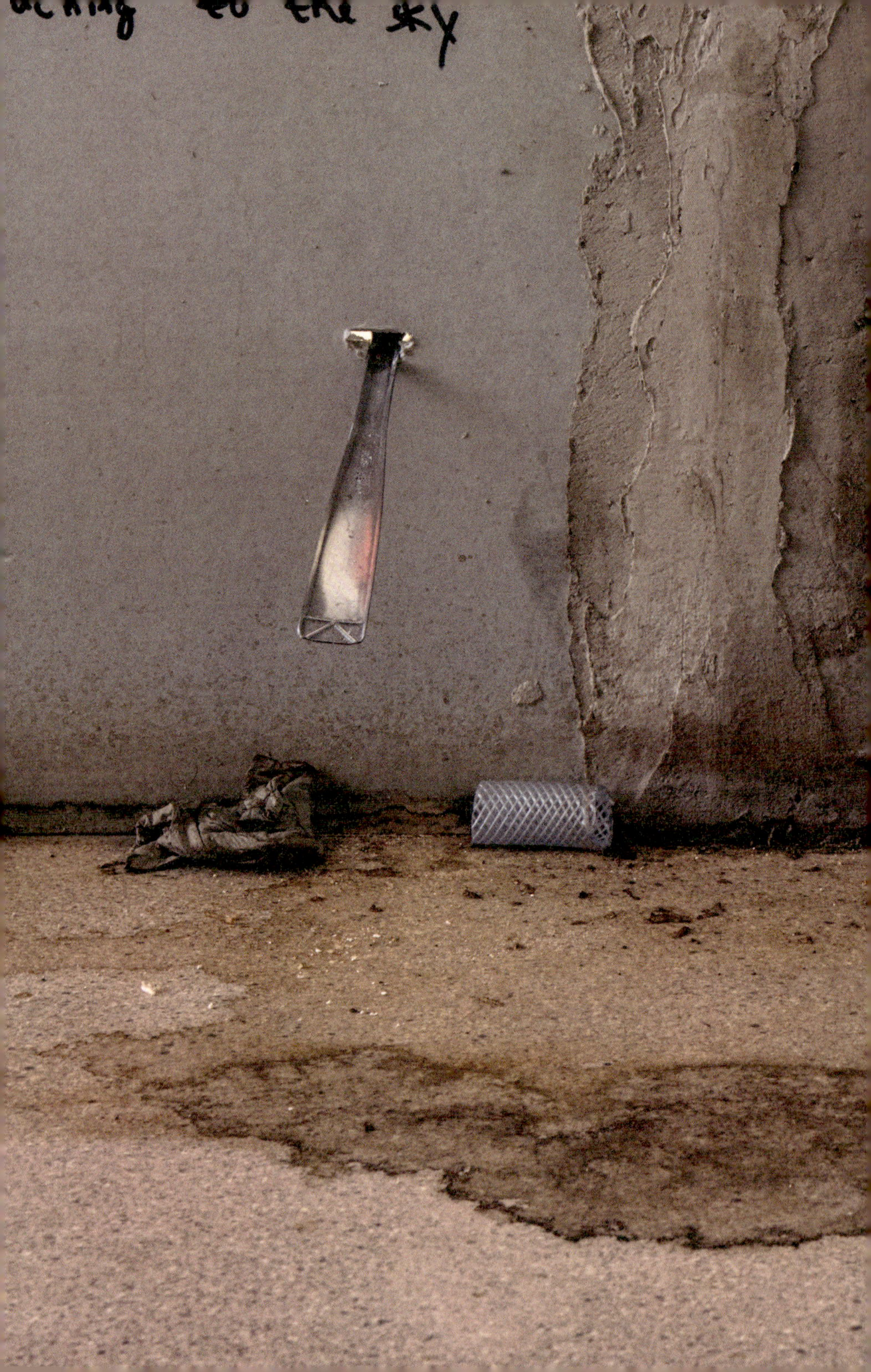
to the sky

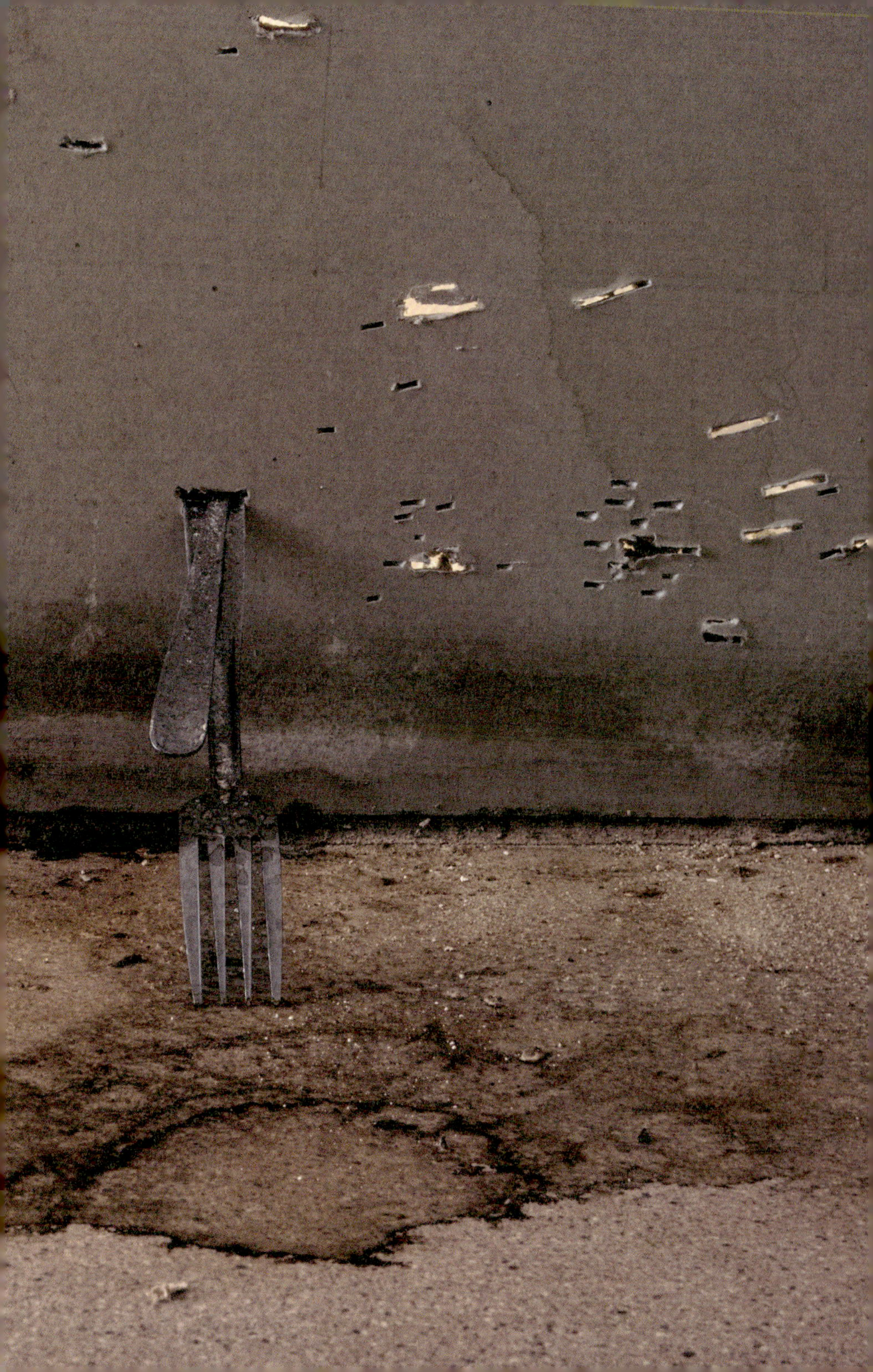

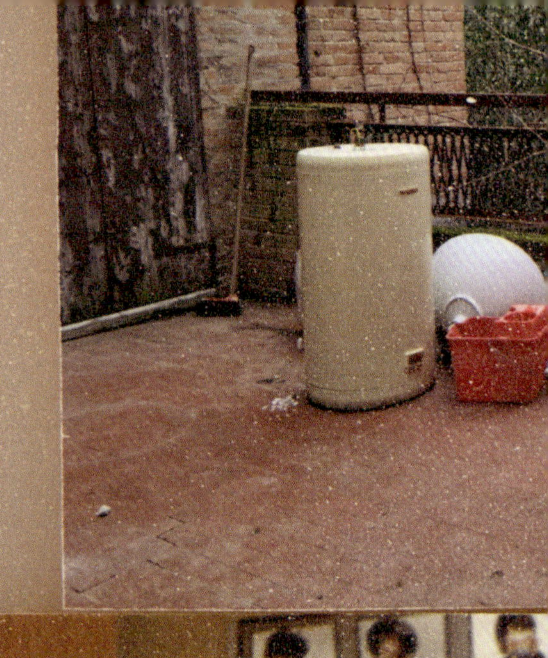

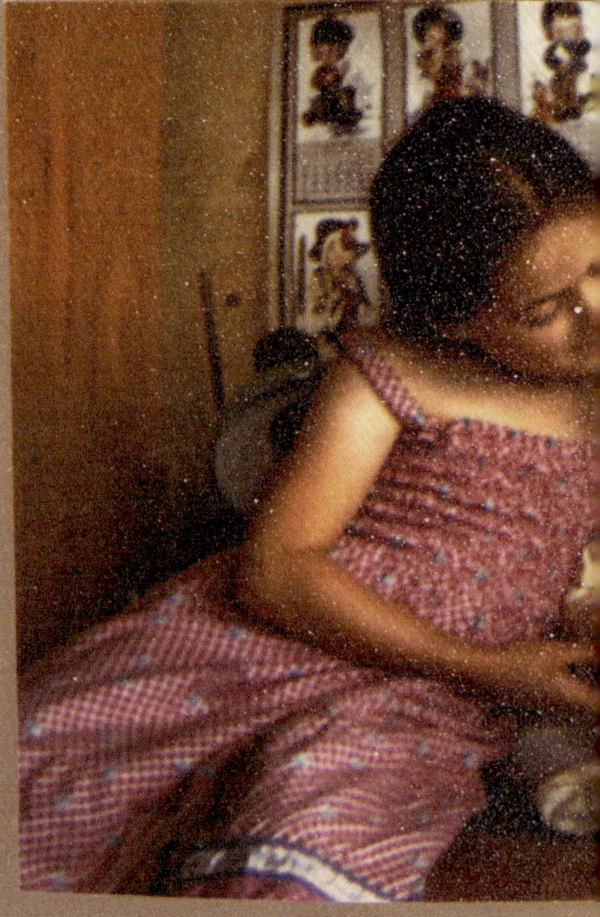

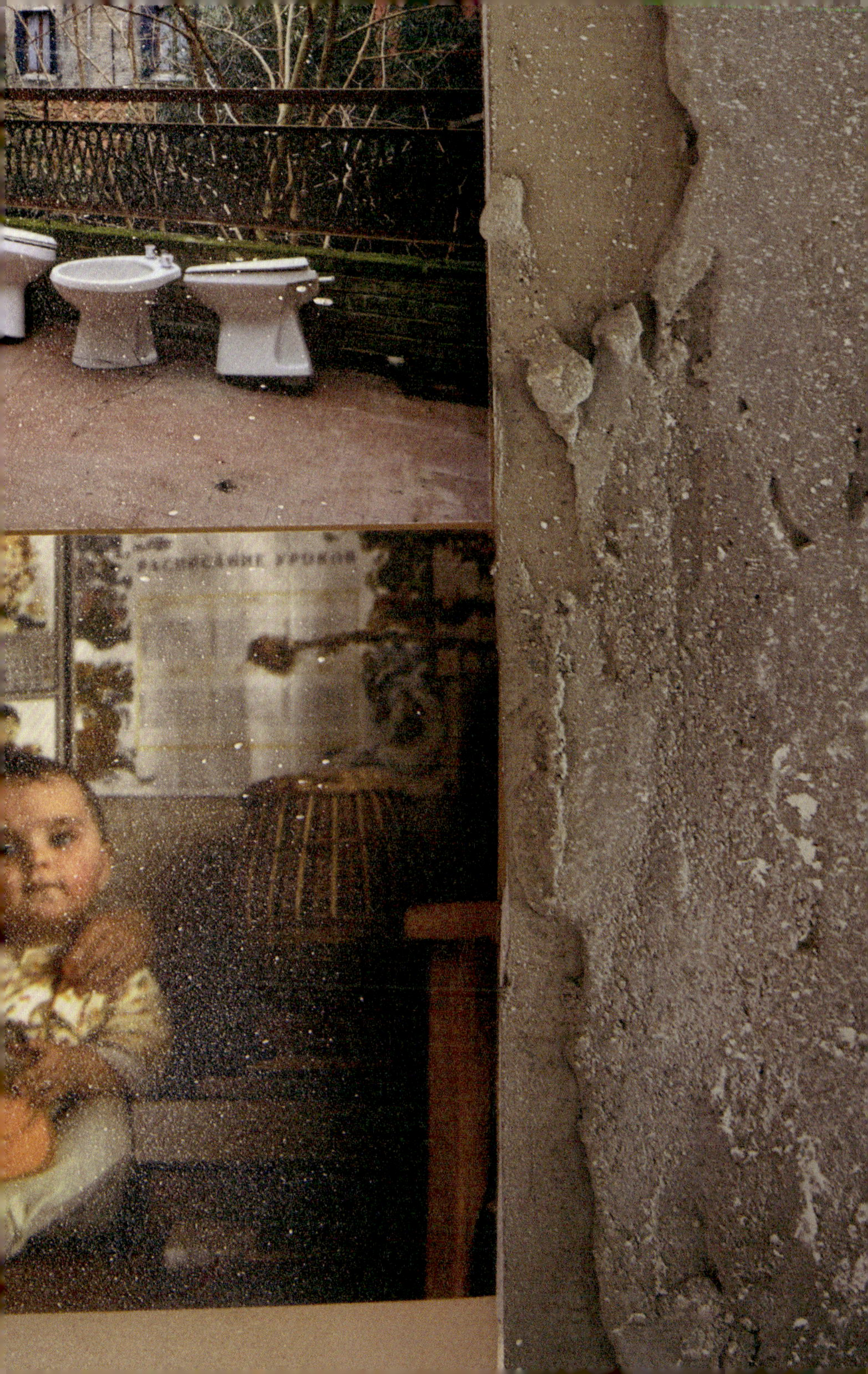

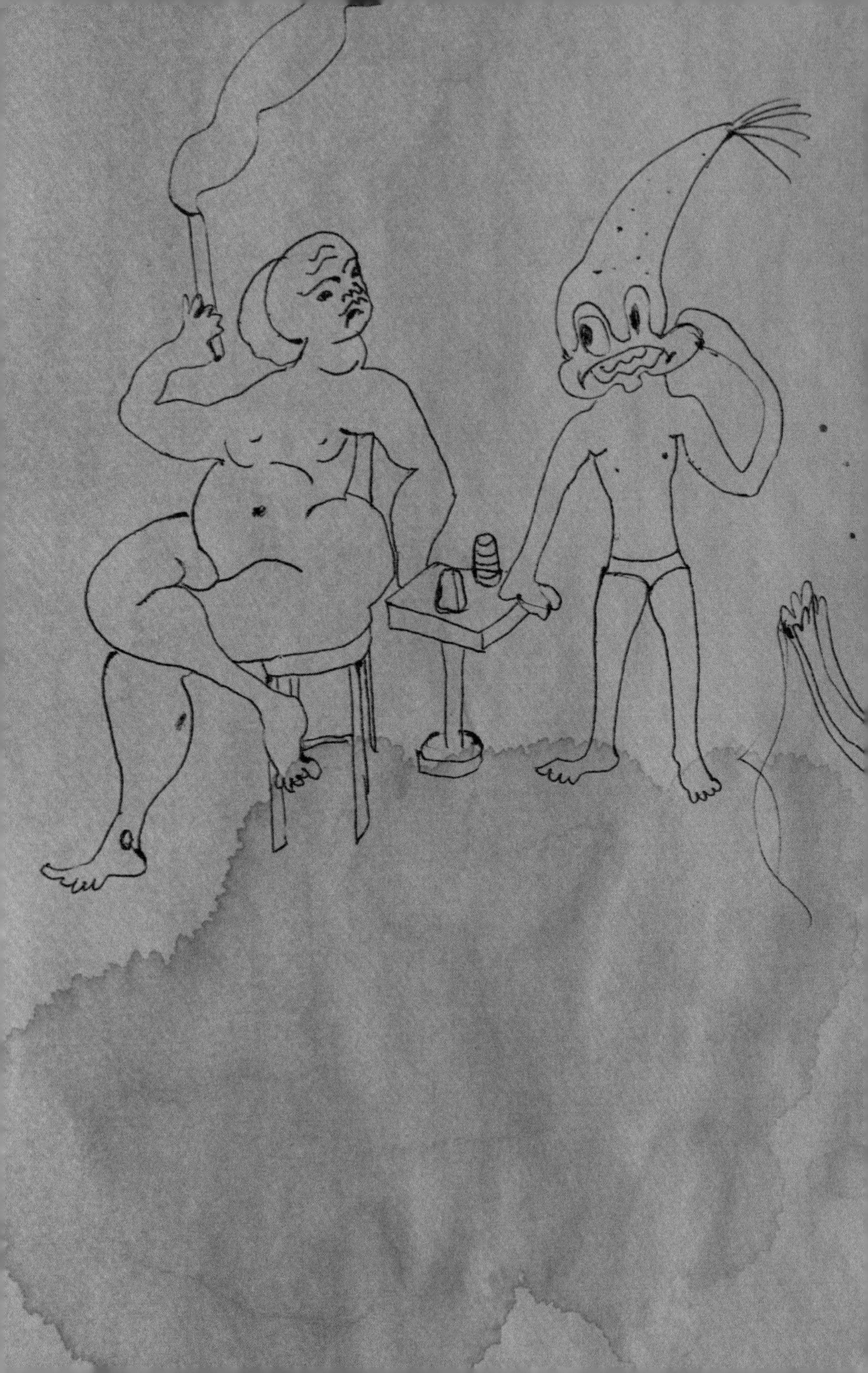

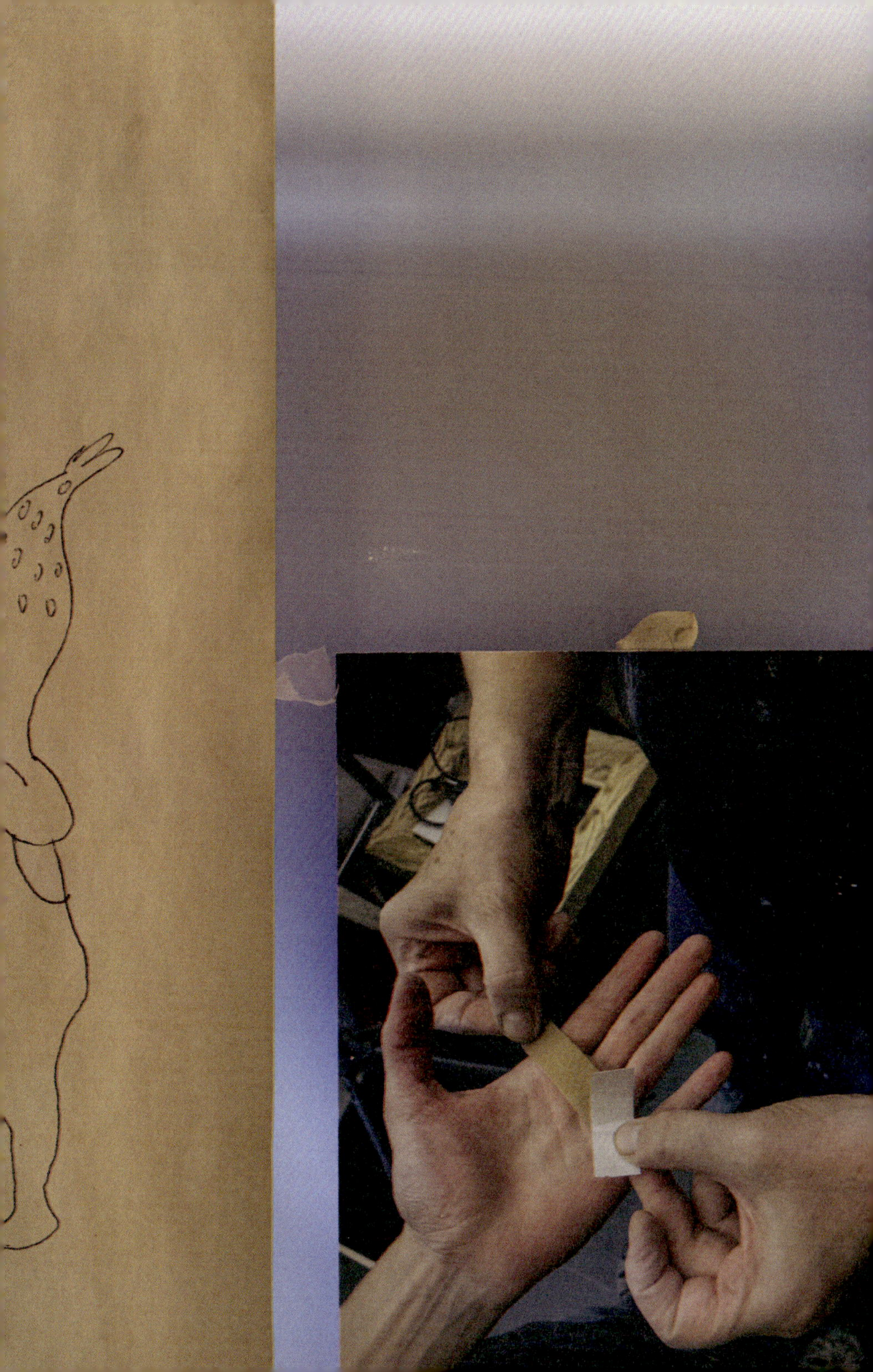

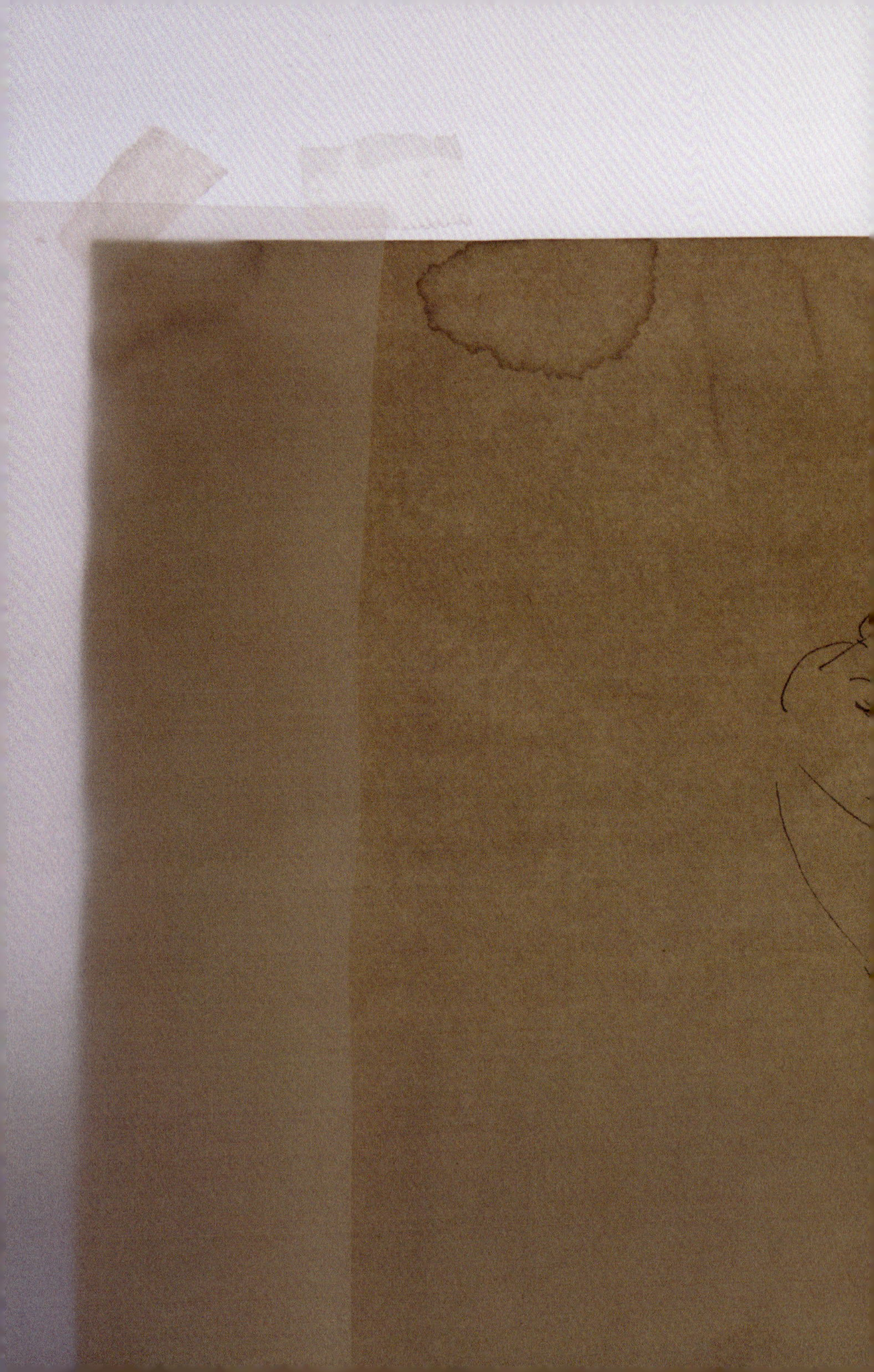

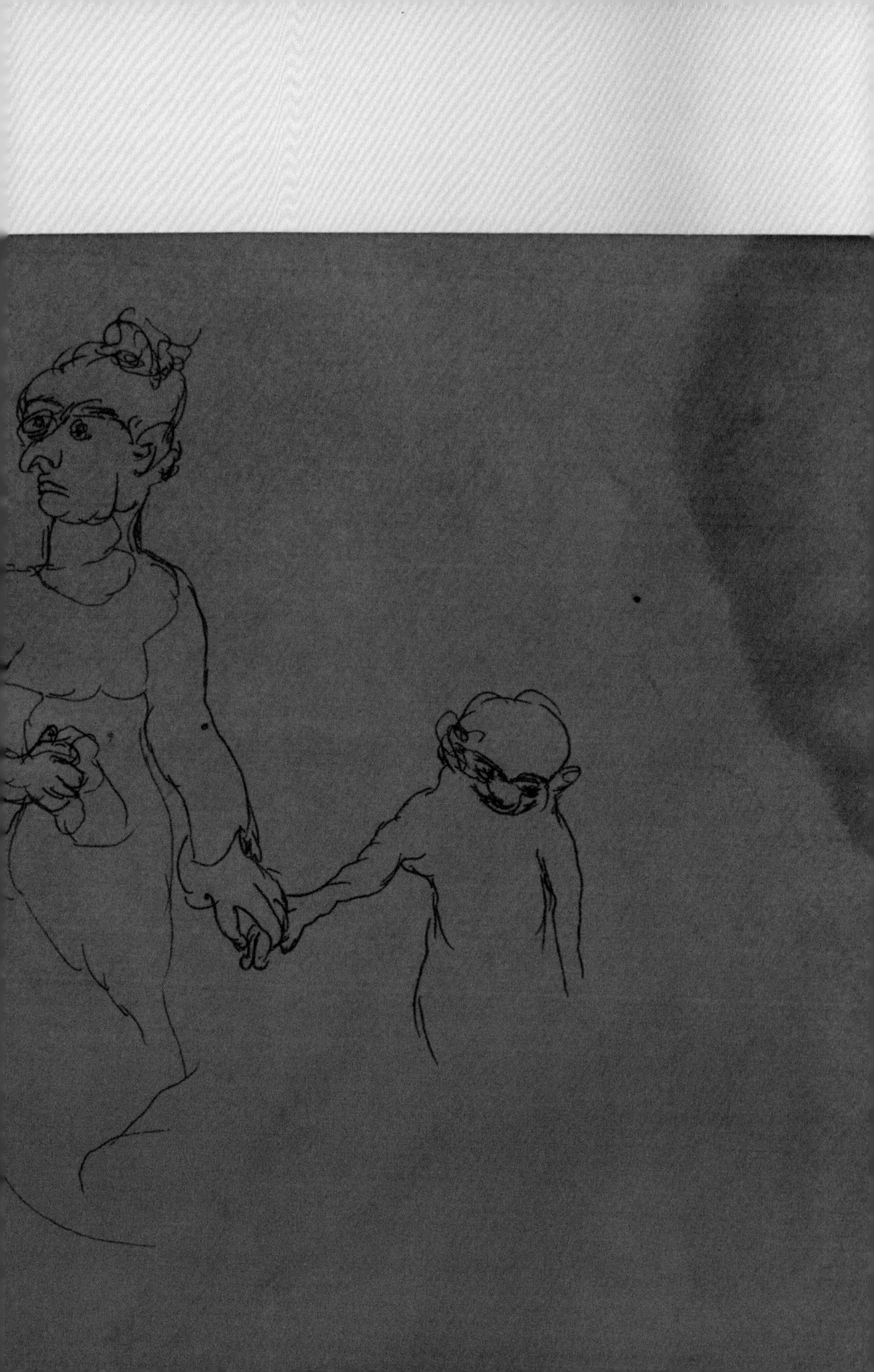

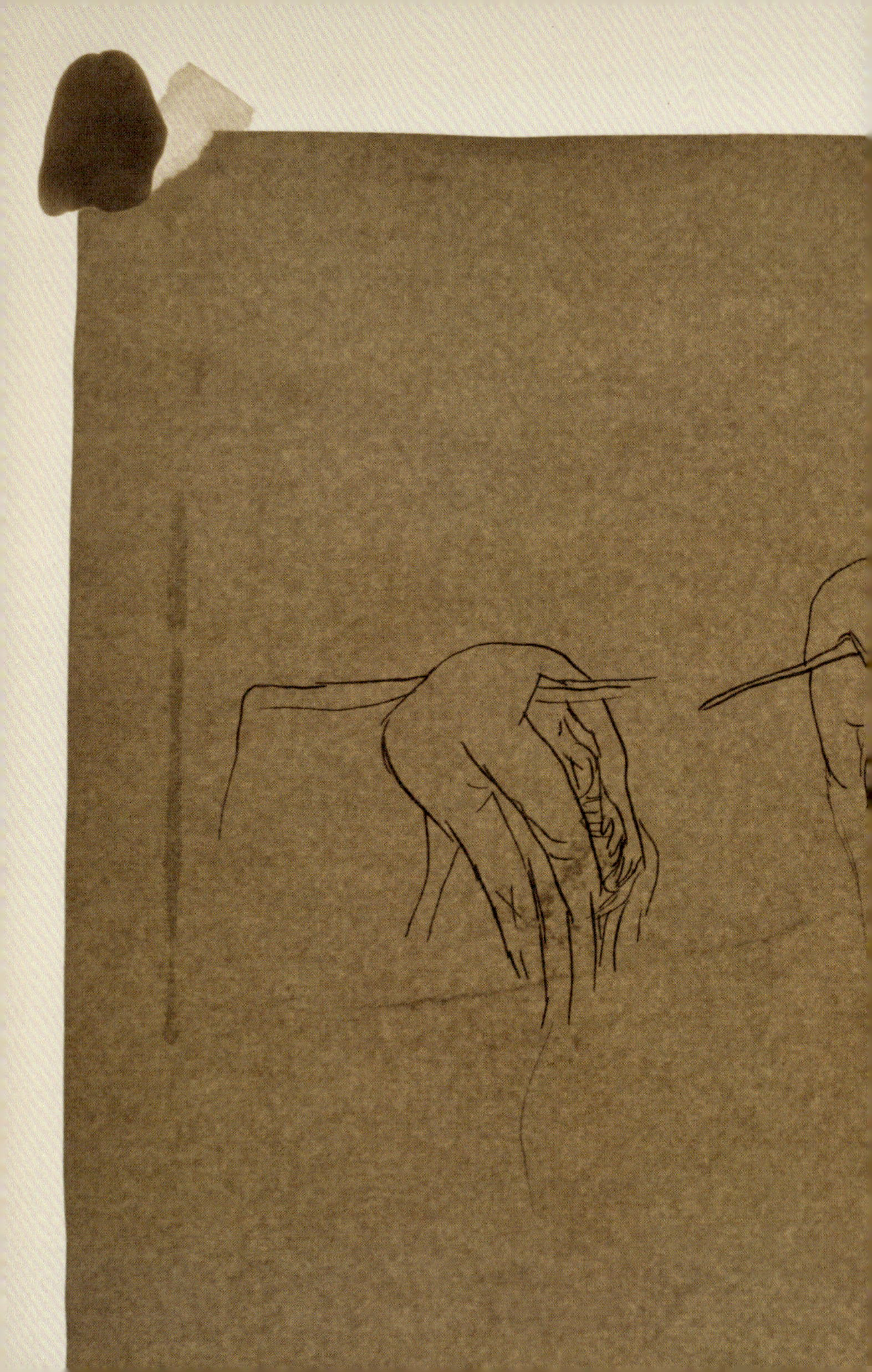

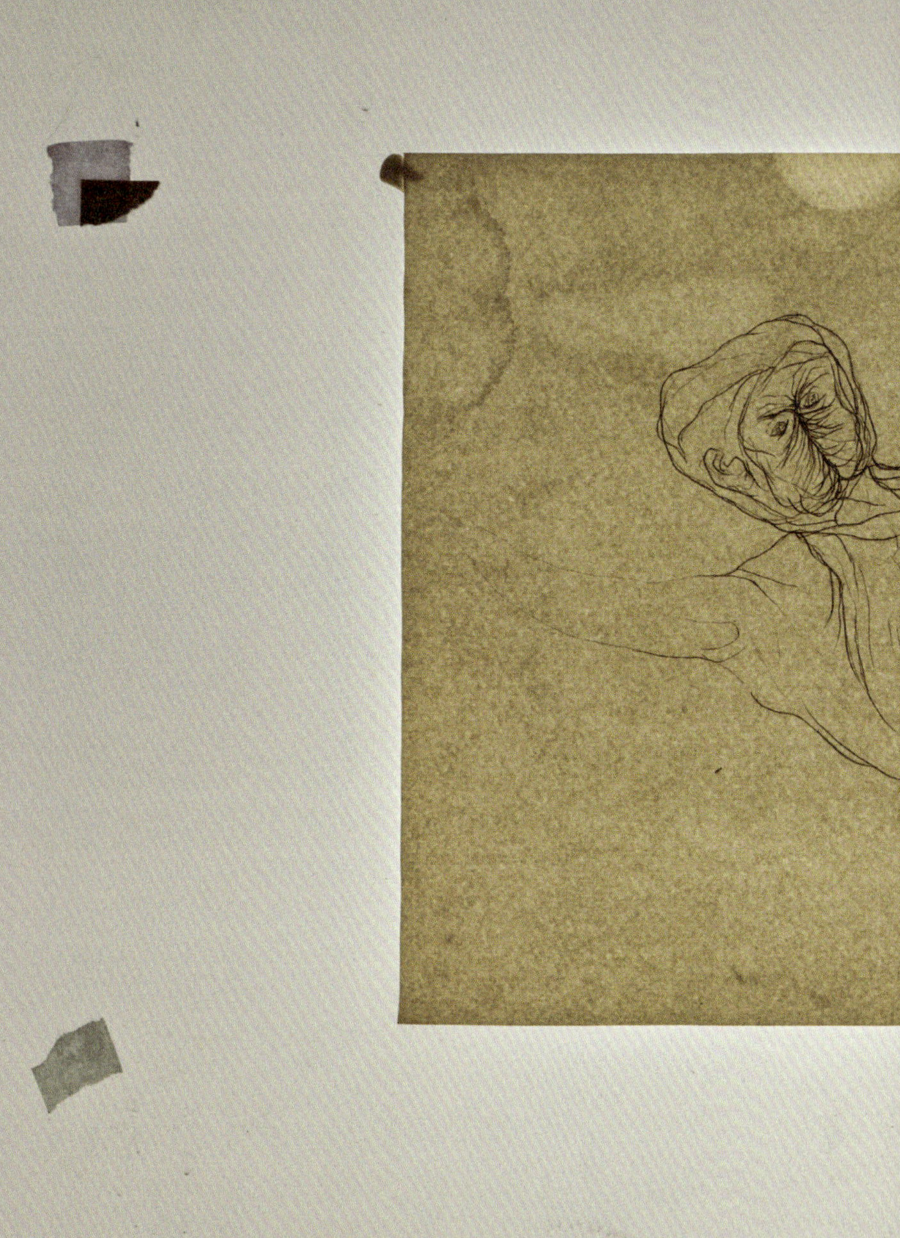

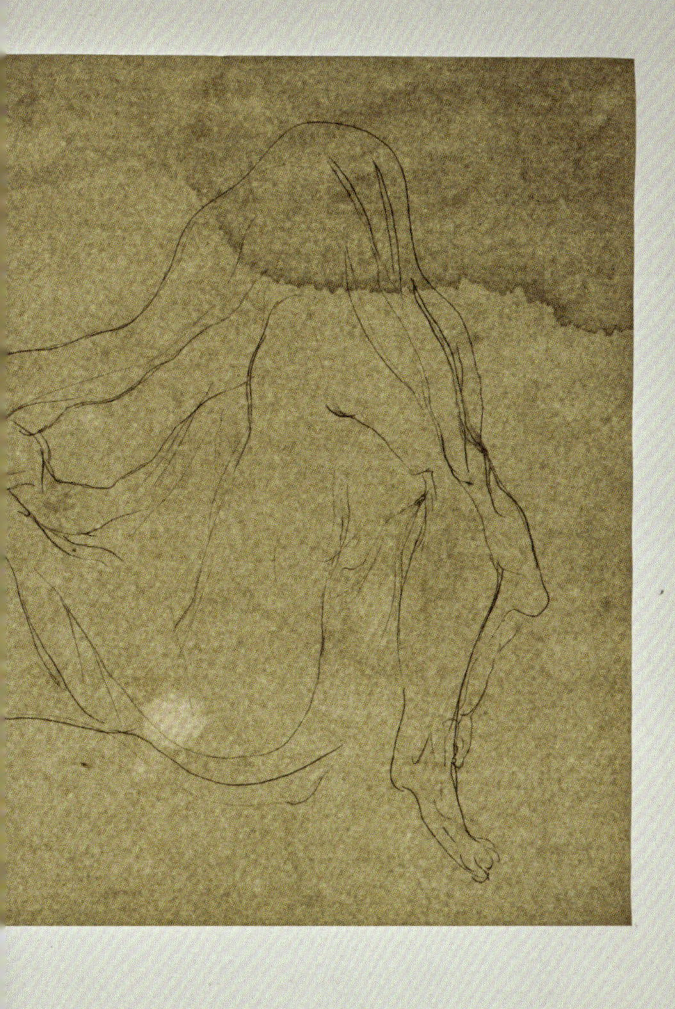

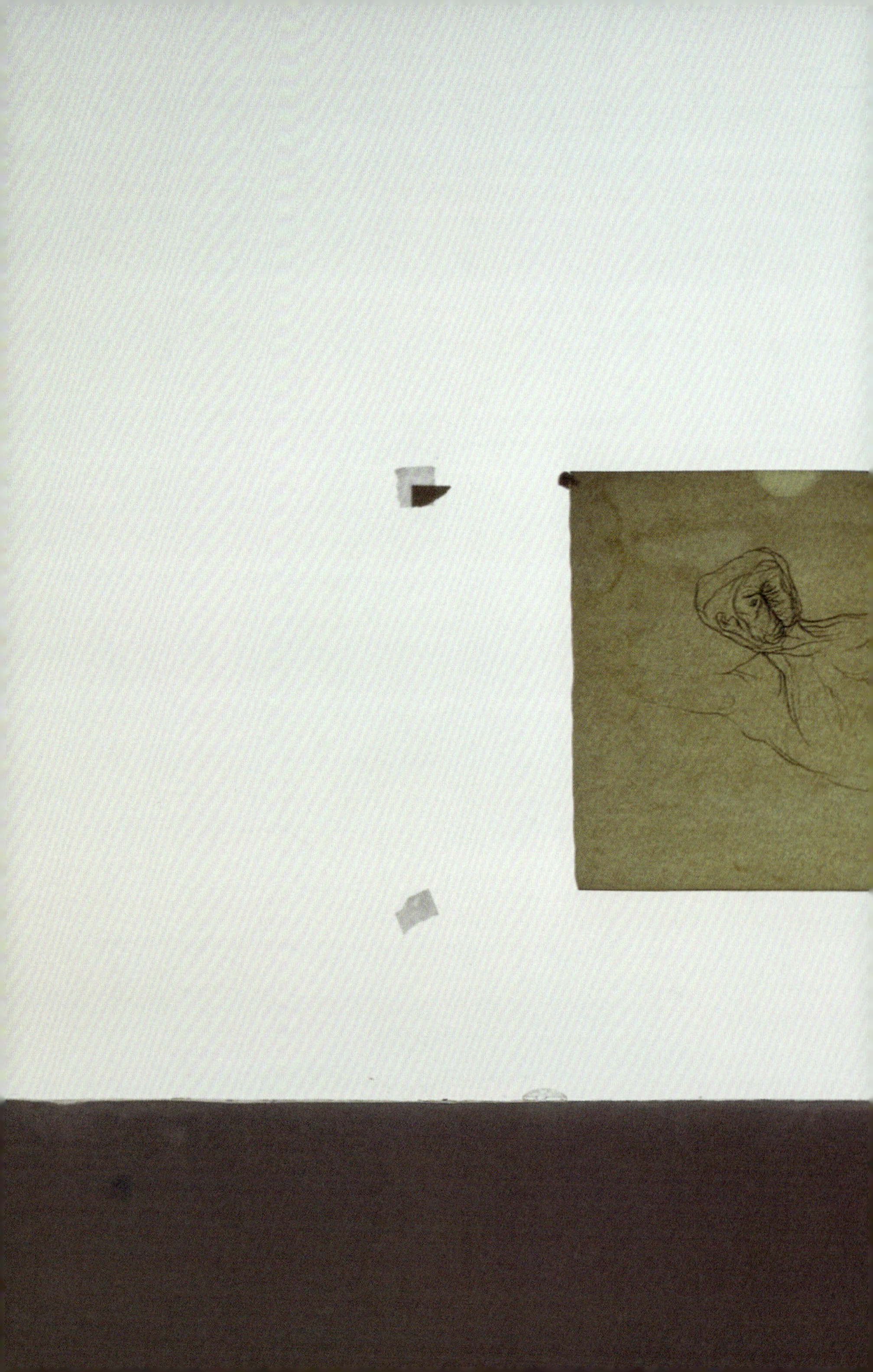

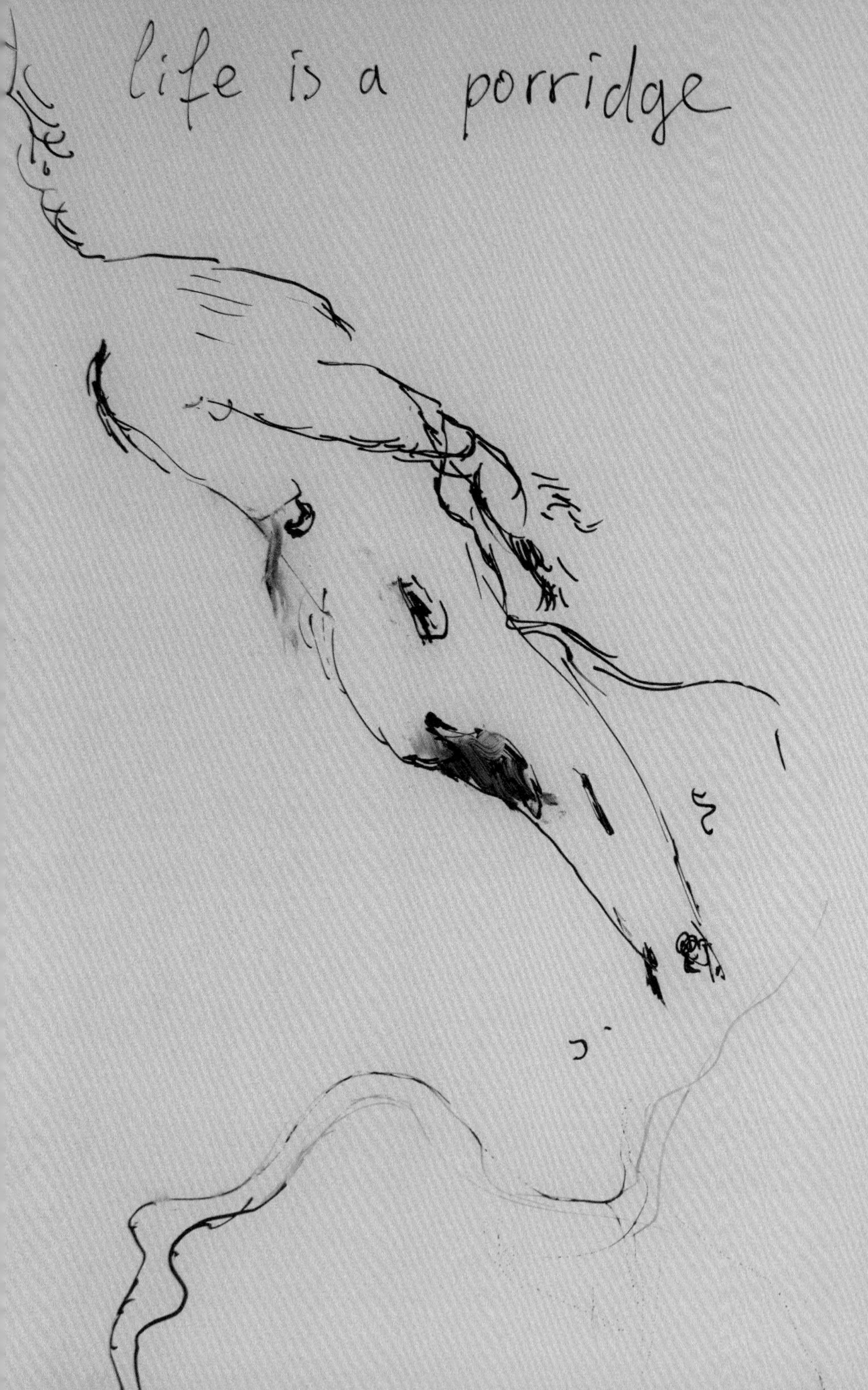
life is a porridge

ook at all wounds
from before
nd from others

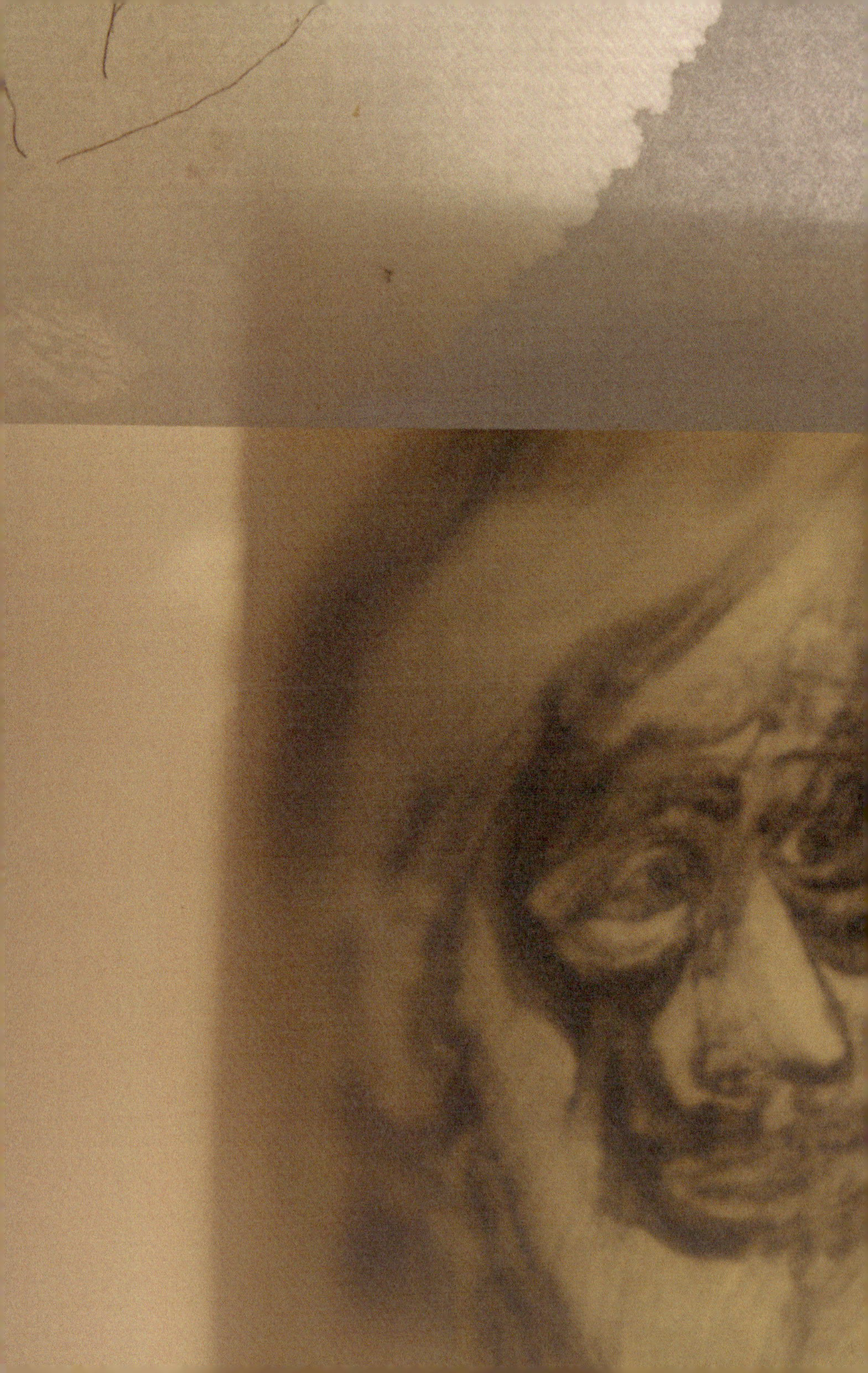

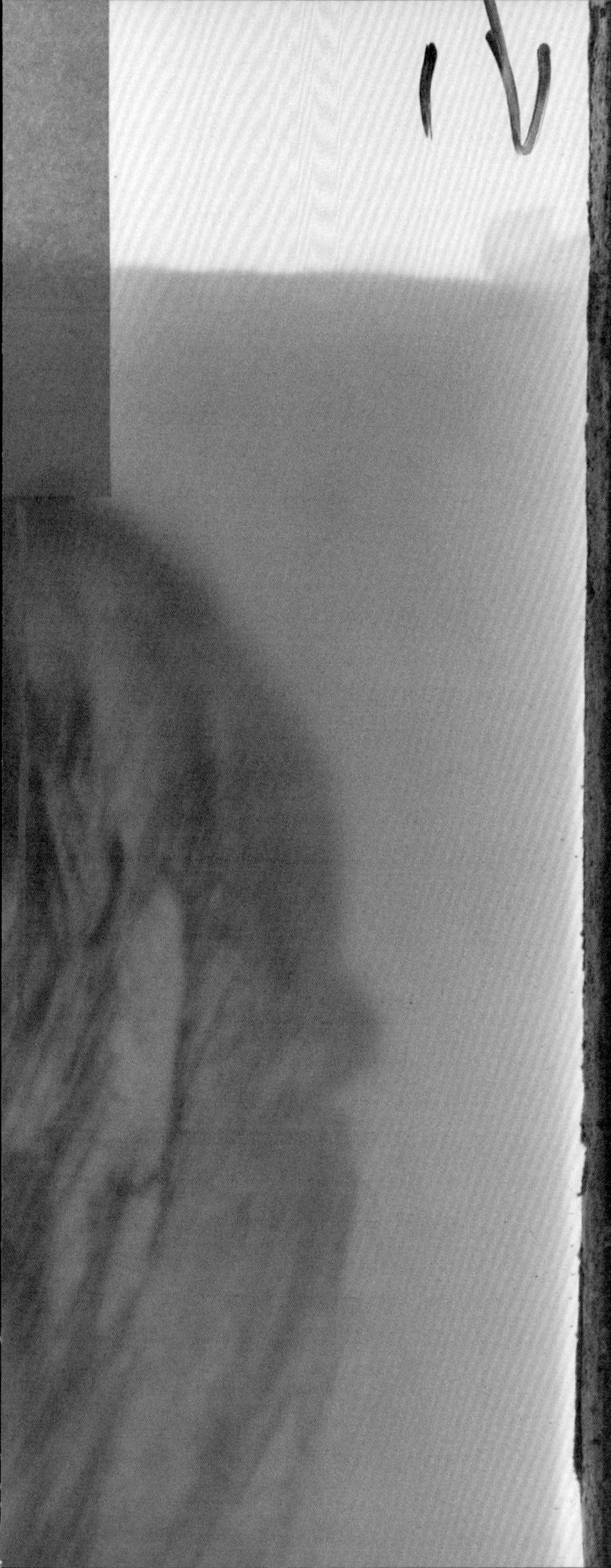

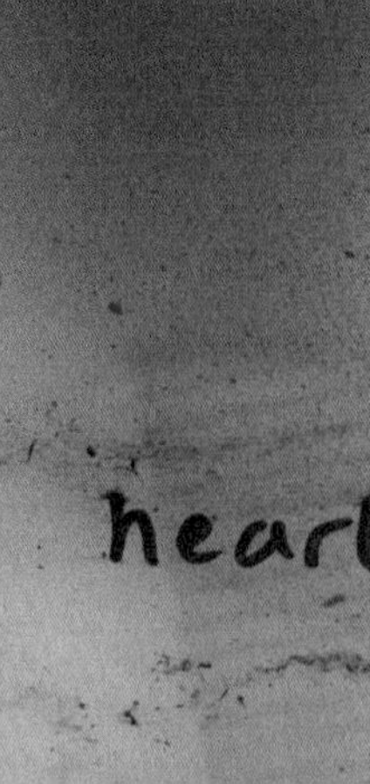

hardened cold

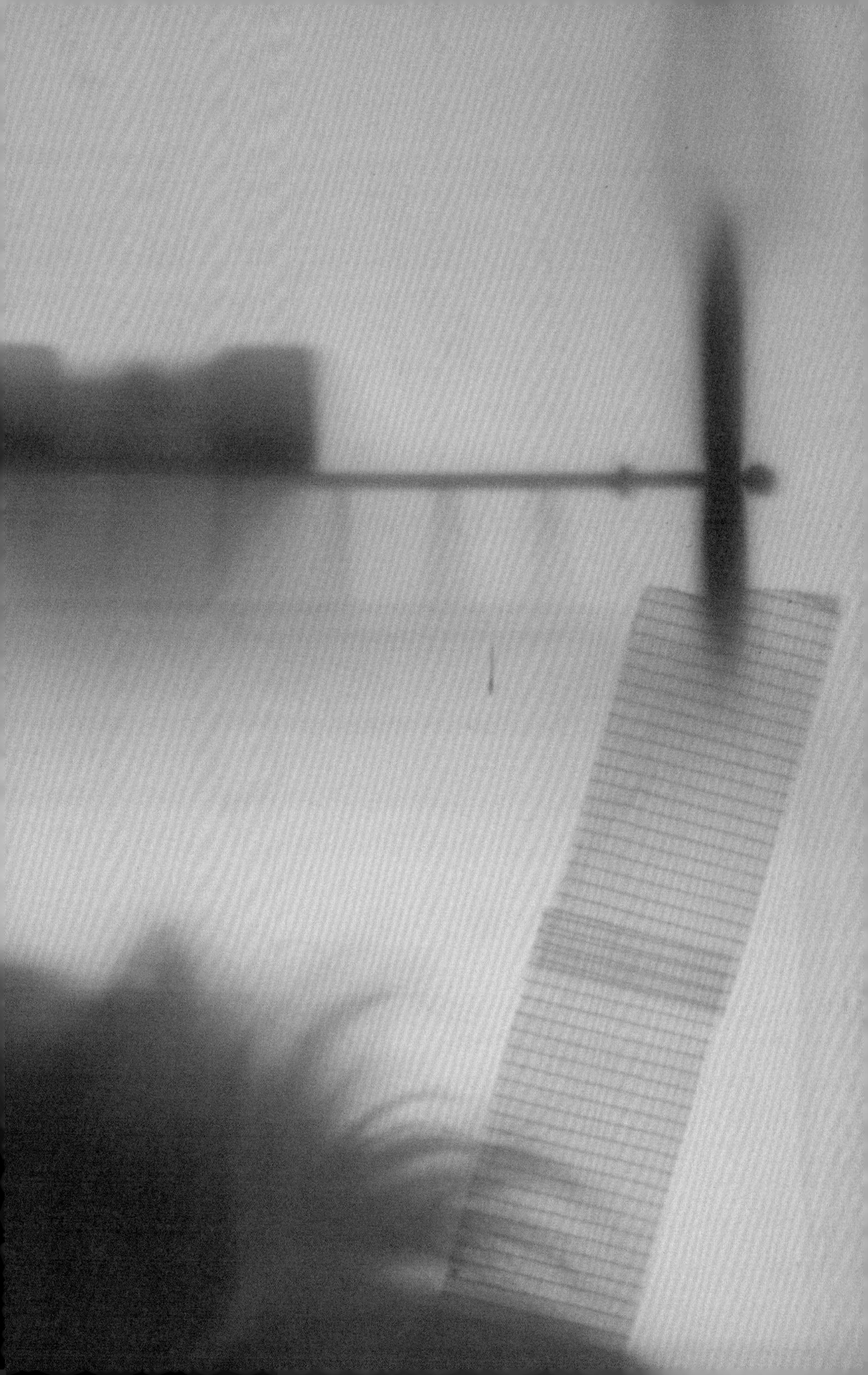

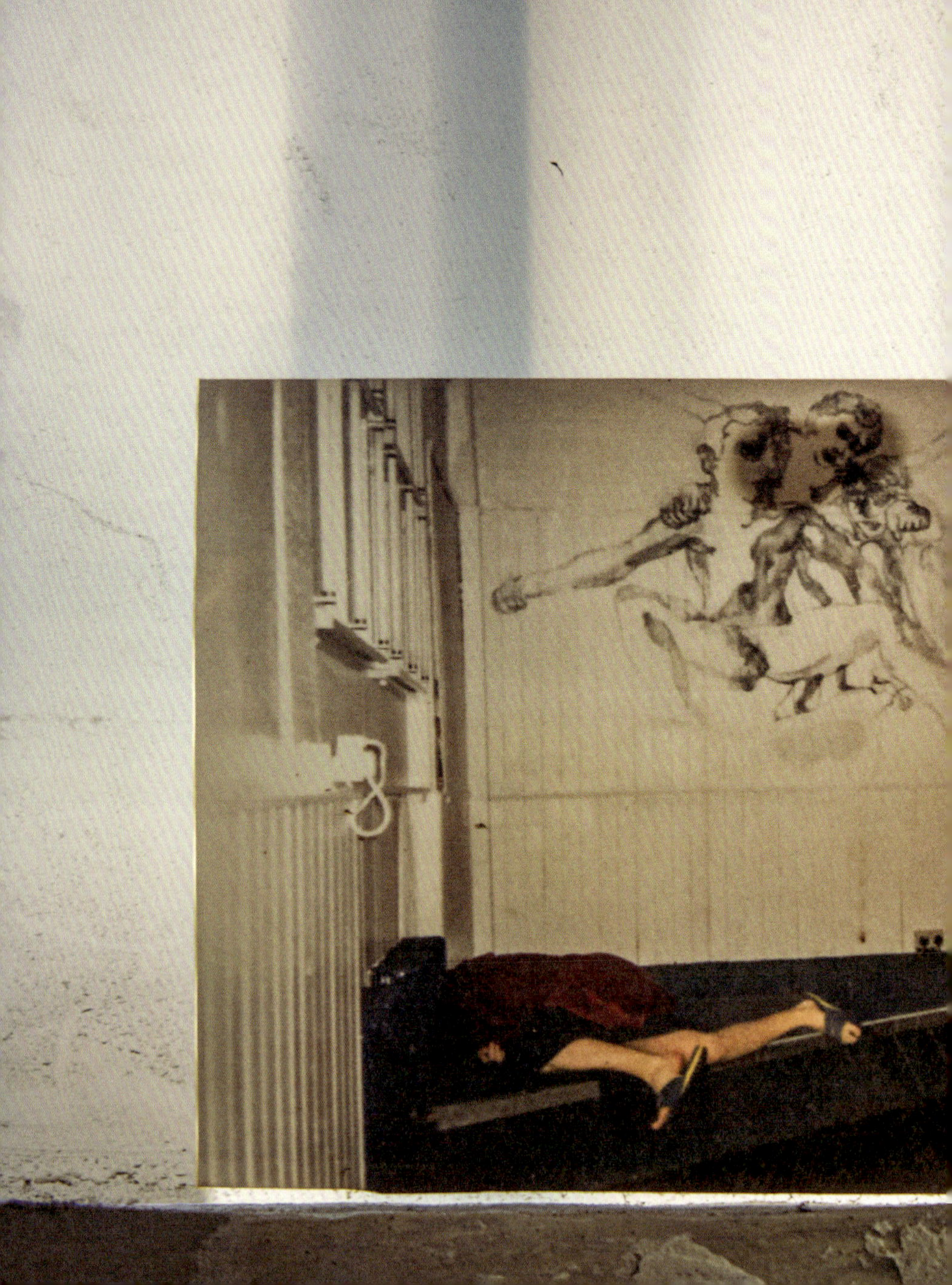

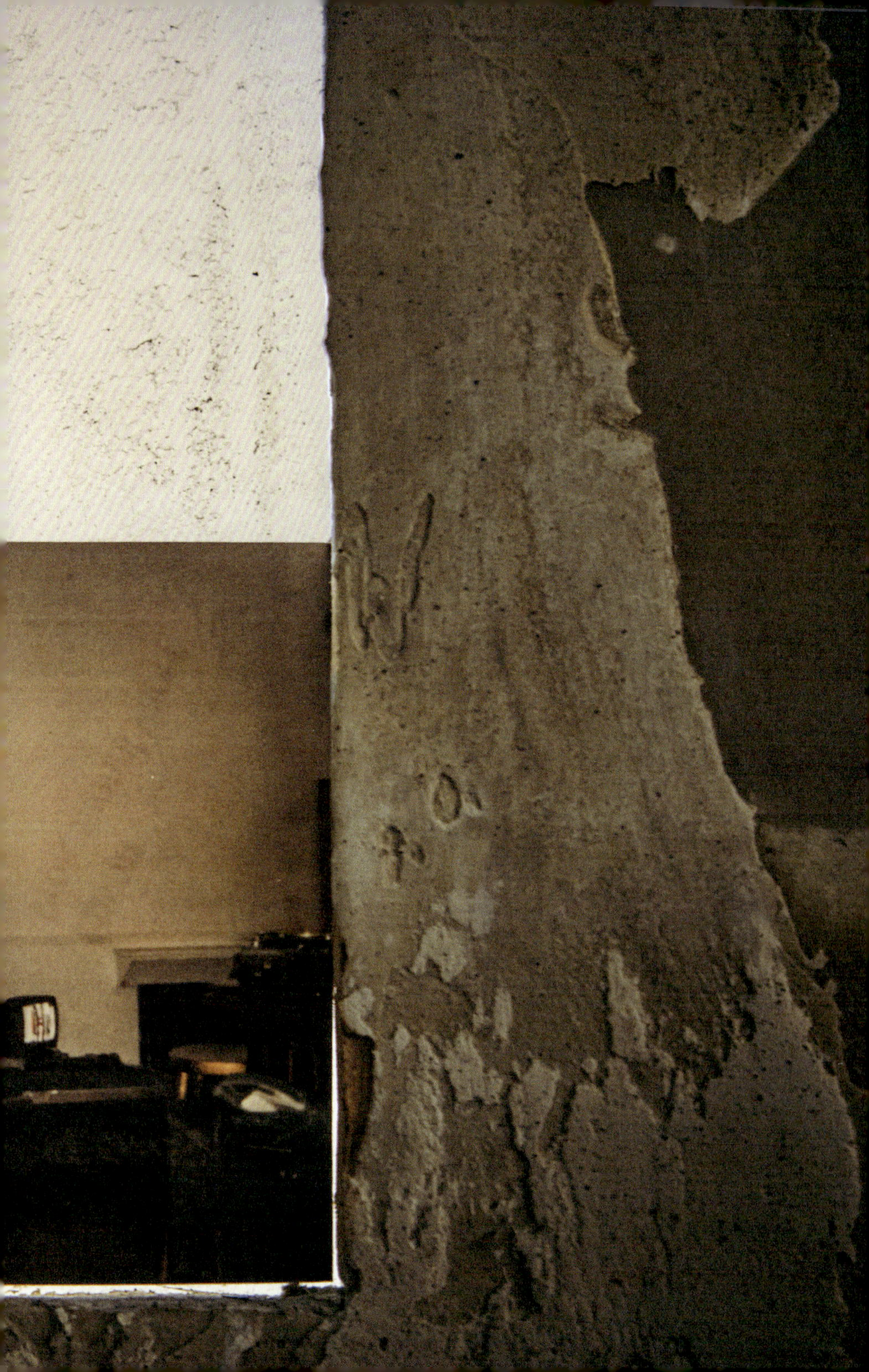

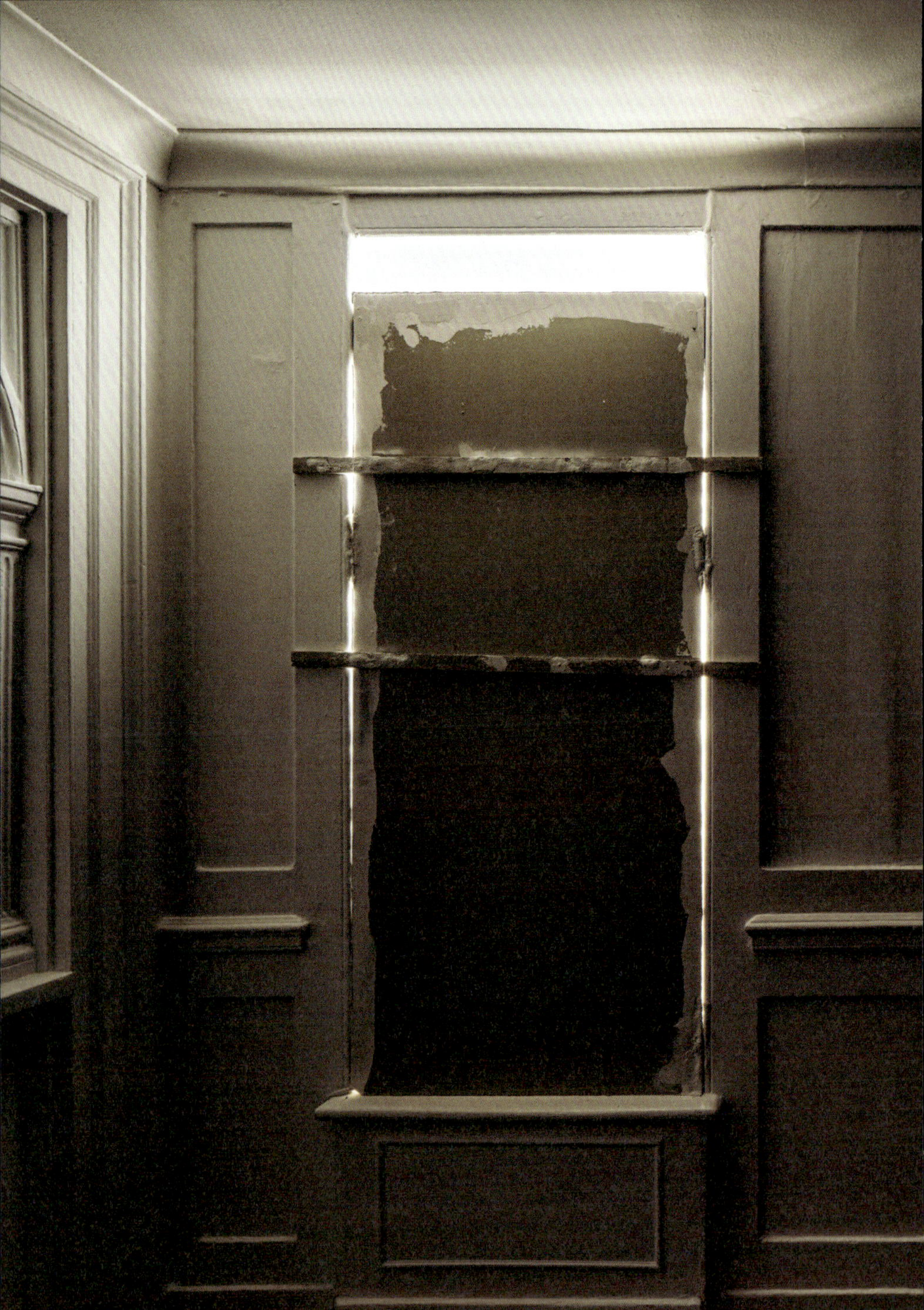

The inevitable everyday of memory

An old woman now
Time passes in memory as deeply now as in the inevitable everyday of breakfast, fiddleheads beginning, the struggle of tugging on my bathing suit. Re-scheduling appointments.Breaking in new shoes.

The emptiness of it all.
Full how full it always is.

Laundry. Buying sugar, butter, safety pins. Reading, reading, thoughts of death flitting. Brushing my teeth again and again. Eating lunch again and again.
The emptiness of it all yet full how full how filled with things with little things.
Filled full with little little things.

And course, then the hulking things that assign labels:
Before. During. After. Never again.

The child. Yes. Waiting. Always waiting. Gone. Gone now. Grown and gone.
Marriage. Yes. One. One done. Two. Two done too.
The child. Yes. Born wet. So loved. So loved. Moving always further further.
Twirling out of reach, then back, then back again twirling gone away again.

And Mother. Father. Their mothers. Their fathers. Their brothers. Their sisters.
And some of their brothers' their sisters' children, too. There. Always there,
Full. So full. Always coming, talking, eating, asking, weeping, leaving.
Now empty packed away in boxes buried in the earth.

The emptiness of it all always and how full how always full
The flotsam. The ephemera. Bits and pieces. Hardly there.

Piles of something hardly barely there.
Piles of this, that or something else. Compelling attention. Demanding inspection.
Today, my father in the car, the smell of dye, a river run red with rouge.
Tomorrow something else again and tonight still dreams manage to confound.

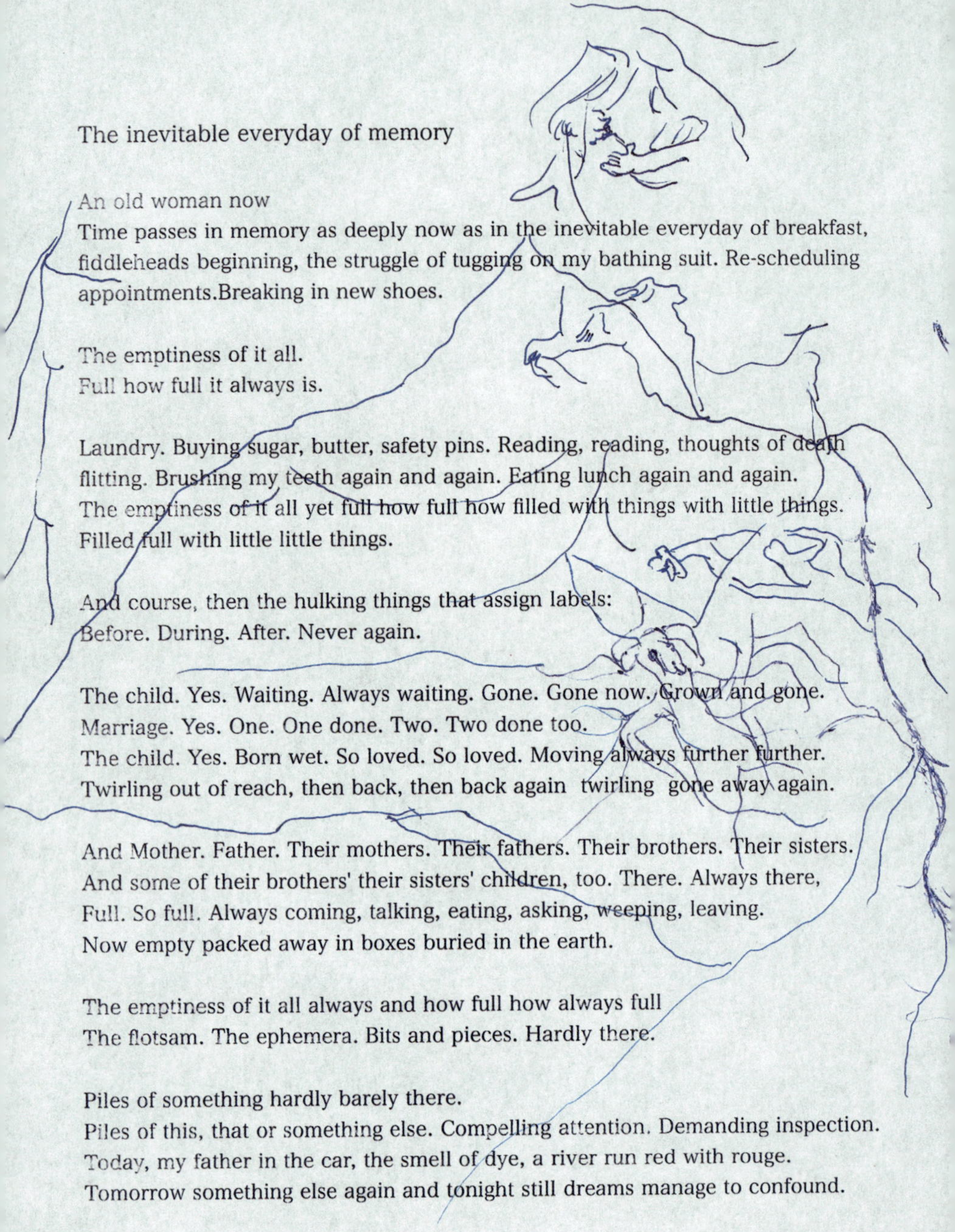

The inevitable everyday of memory

An old woman now
Time passes in memory as deeply now as in the inevitable everyday of breakfast,
fiddleheads beginning, the struggle of tugging on my bathing suit. Re-scheduling
appointments.Breaking in new shoes.

The emptiness of it all.
Full how full it always is.

Laundry. Buying sugar, butter, safety pins. Reading, reading, thoughts of death
flitting. Brushing my teeth again and again. Eating lunch again and again.
The emptiness of it all yet full how full how filled with things with little things.
Filled full with little little things.

And course, then the hulking things that assign labels:
Before. During. After. Never again.

The child. Yes. Waiting. Always waiting. Gone. Gone now. Grown and gone.
Marriage. Yes. One. One done. Two. Two done too.
The child. Yes. Born wet. So loved. So loved. Moving always further further.
Twirling out of reach, then back, then back again twirling gone away again.

And Mother. Father. Their mothers. Their fathers. Their brothers. Their sisters.
And some of their brothers' their sisters' children, too. There. Always there,
Full. So full. Always coming, talking, eating, asking, weeping, leaving.
Now empty packed away in boxes buried in the earth.

The emptiness of it all always and how full how always full
The flotsam. The ephemera. Bits and pieces. Hardly there.

Piles of something hardly barely there.
Piles of this, that or something else. Compelling attention. Demanding inspection.
Today, my father in the car, the smell of dye, a river run red with rouge.
Tomorrow something else again and tonight still dreams manage to confound.

Text Livia Polanyi
Drawings Tolia Astakhishvili

I sit here in my chair
imagining now the seconds, minutes,
heartbeats of an imagined now
dissolving into a common then
as you read what I am writing now.

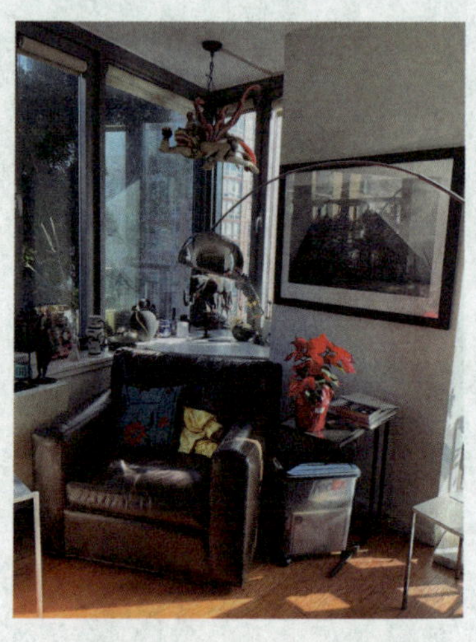

Remembering now being in bed this morning

remembering standing in a space then
looking at a small drawing that imagined that
space in a future that then was now

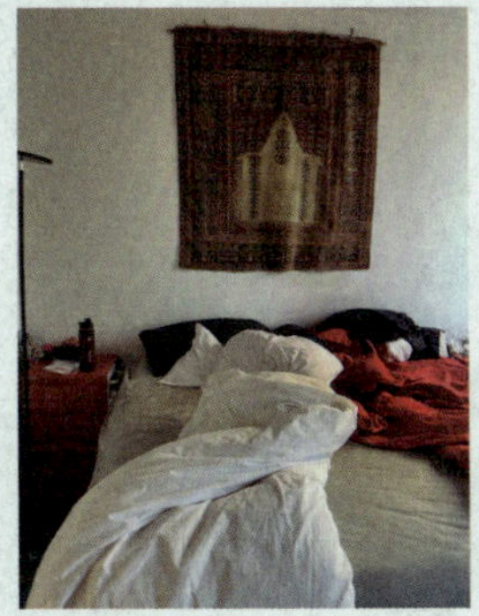

E-mail from Livia Polanyi

Tolia Astakhishvili (b. 1974, Tbilisi, GE) lives and works in Berlin, DE, and Tbilisi, GE. Upcoming solo exhibition at Mumok, Vienna, AT (2026). Previous recent solo exhibitions include *a wound on my plate*, Emalin, London, GB, and *to love and devour*, Nicoletta Fiorucci Foundation, Venice, IT (2025); *Result*, LC Queisser, Tbilisi, GE; *between father and mother*, SculptureCenter, New York, US (2024); *The First Finger (chapter II)*, and Haus am Waldsee, Berlin, DE (2023); *The First Finger*, Bonner Kunstverein, Bonn, DE (2023); *I Think It's Closed*, Bielefeld Kunstverein, Bielefeld, DE (2023).

Her work has been included in exhibitions at Para Site, Hong Kong (2026); the 15th Kaunas Biennial, Kaunas, LT; Fondation Pernod Ricard, Paris, FR; MoMA PS1, New York, US (2025); MACRO Museum, Rome, IT; LC Queisser, Tbilisi, GE; galerie frank elbaz, Paris, FR; Condo Complex, London, GB (2024); Kunsthalle Zürich, Zurich, CH; Emalin, London, GB; Molitor Gallery, Berlin, DE; LC Queisser, Tbilisi, GE (2023); Shahin Zarinbal, Berlin, DE; Felix Gaudlitz, Vienna, AT; LC Queisser, Tbilisi, GE (2022); Art Hub Copenhagen, Copenhagen, DK; Räume für Kunst, Kerpen, DE; Bonner Kunstverein, Bonn, DE; Capitain Petzel, Berlin, DE (2021); Malmö Konsthall, Malmö, SE (2019); Cabinet, London, GB (2018).

Jackson Bein (b. Louisiana, US; lives/works in New York, US) is an artist and writer interested in embodiment, individuation, and limits. Bein graduated from The Cooper Union (2024) with the Jacques and Natasha Gelman Foundation Prize and Fred V. Lane Award. Recent fellowships and residencies include: the Durational Pedagogies Fellowship at Dia Chelsea (2025–6); the Prepared Table Fellowship at Rivers Institute for Contemporary Art & Thought with the Amistad Research Center (2025); the Benjamin Menschel Creative Inquiry Fellowship (2024); Craft 101 at Arts Letters and Numbers (2024); SimShip Studios at Arts Letters and Numbers (2023); and the Critical Philosophy certificate program at The New Centre for Research & Practice (2024–5). Bein operates the project space Interrobang H232 in Brooklyn, New York, US.

Livia Polanyi is a linguist who has taught at a few universities and worked at a few Silicon Valley research labs. The author of *Telling the American Story*, a scholarly underground cult volume published by the MIT Press, has always done her own thing and been amazed that she got paid for it. She once had a brief affair with performance art in the Netherlands in the 1980s and did a gig at The Kitchen in the 2000s. She is the subject of a short film shot mostly aloft in a zeppelin, in which she mentioned woolly mammoths. She holds twenty-two US patents. She has been married three times, is very old, and lives contentedly in New York City in the middle of the East River with her beloved third and final. She owns a 1903 Edison cylinder machine and a few cylinders. They are a little wonky but still play. She does not have a cat and does not eat cabbage, garlic, or spicy foods. She is bewildered that she likes Kimchee and by how it has all turned out.

Biographies

Tolia Astakhishvili (b. 1974, Tbilisi, GE) lives and works in Berlin, DE, and Tbilisi, GE. Upcoming solo exhibition at Mumok, Vienna, AT (2026). Previous, recent solo exhibitions include *a wound on my plate*, Emalin, London, GB, and *to love and devour*, Nicoletta Fiorucci Foundation, Venice, IT (2025); *Result*, LC Queisser, Tbilisi, GE; *between father and mother*, SculptureCenter, New York, US (2024); *The First Finger (chapter II)*, and Haus am Waldsee, Berlin, DE (2023); *The First Finger*, Bonner Kunstverein, Bonn, DE (2023); *I Think It's Closed*, Bielefeld Kunstverein, Bielefeld, DE (2023).

Her work has been included in exhibitions at Para Site, Hong-Kong (2026); the 15th Kaunas Biennial, Kaunas, LT; Fondation Pernod Ricard, Paris, FR; MoMA PS1, New York, US (2025); MACRO Museum, Rome, IT; LC Queisser, Tbilisi, GE; galerie frank elbaz, Paris, FR; Condo Complex, London, GB (2024); Kunsthalle Zürich, Zurich, CH; Emalin, London, GB; Molitor Gallery, Berlin, DE; LC Queisser, Tbilisi, GE (2023); Shahin Zarinbal, Berlin, DE; Felix Gaudlitz, Vienna, AT; LC Queisser, Tbilisi, GE (2022); Art Hub Copenhagen, Copenhagen, DK; Räume für Kunst, Kerpen, DE; Bonner Kunstverein, Bonn, DE; Capitain Petzel, Berlin, DE (2021); Malmö Konsthall, Malmö, SE (2019); Cabinet, London, GB (2018).

Jacksun Bein (b. Louisiana, US; lives/works in New York, US) is an artist and writer interested in embodiment, individuation, and limits. Bein graduated from The Cooper Union (2024) with the Jacques and Natasha Gelman Foundation Prize and Fred A. Lane Award. Recent fellowships and residencies include: the Durational Pedagogies Fellowship at Dia Chelsea (2025–6); the Prepared Table Fellowship at Rivers Institute for Contemporary Art & Thought with the Amistad Research Center (2023); the Benjamin Menschel Creative Inquiry Fellowship (2024); Craft 101 at Arts Letters and Numbers (2024); SunShip Studios at Arts Letters and Numbers (2023); and the Critical Philosophy certificate program at The New Centre for Research & Practice (2024–5). Bein operates the project space Interrobang 11232 in Brooklyn, New York, US.

Livia Polanyi is a linguist who has taught at a few universities and worked at a few Silicon Valley research labs. The author of *Telling the American Story*, a scholarly underground cult volume published by the MIT Press, has always done her own thing and been amazed that she got paid for it. She once had a brief affair with performance art in the Netherlands in the 1980s and did a gig at The Kitchen in the 2010s. She is the subject of a short film shot mostly aloft in a zeppelin, in which she mentioned woolly mammoths. She holds twenty-two US patents. She has been married three times, is very old, and lives contentedly in New York City in the middle of the East River with her beloved third and final. She owns a 1903 Edison cylinder machine and a few cylinders. They are a little wonky but still play. She does not have a cat and does not eat cabbage, garlic, or spicy foods. She is bewildered that she likes kimchee and by how it has all turned out.

KONTEXT—a series by DISTANZ.

Acknowledgments

Matthias Kliefoth and Tolia Astakhishvili thank Jacksun Bein, Livia Polanyi, and Annie Hägg. Additional thanks to Tolia's galleries Emalin and LC Queisser, as well as Zurab Astakhishvili, Geraldine Barton, Goran Chanter, Nikoloz Chkhaidze, Lucy Cowling, Christiane Eggers, Mathilde Labuthie, Nika Lelashvili, Milo Kester, Karlina Mezecka, Oliver Offord, Lisa Offermann, Dylan Peirce, James Richards, Ivan Robirosa, Katie Tomlinson, Leopold Thun, Angelina Volk, Benedict Winkler, Tamusa Zarkua, Michaela Züge-Bruton.

All images, Tolia Astakhishvili, *nearly hardened cold, between the legs, My year of rest and relaxation III*, exhibited as part of *A wound on my plate*, Emalin, London, 2025

Imprint

Editor
Matthias Kliefoth

Design
Mali Wychodil

Design Concept KONTEXT
Manuel Tayarani

Text
Jacksun Bein and Livia Polanyi

Proofreading
Amy Klement

Image Editing
max-color, Berlin

Production
Marcus Sabsch

Printing and Binding
Druckhaus Sportflieger, Berlin

ISBN 978-3-95476-750-2

Printed in Germany

Published by
DISTANZ Verlag
www.distanz.de